BY THE BRIDGE OR BY THE RIVER?

AMY C. ROMA

STORIES OF IMMIGRATION
FROM THE SOUTHERN BORDER

C&R Press
Conscious & Responsible

First Edition
1 2 3 4 5 6 7 8 9

Cover art *xxx*
Interior design by Jojo Rita

ISBN: xxx
LCCN: xxx

C&R Press
Conscious & Responsible
crpress.org

For special discounted bulk purchases, please contact:
C&R Press sales@crpress.org
Contact info@crpress.org to book events, readings and author signings.

BY THE BRIDGE OR
BY THE RIVER?

Contents

v   *Prologue*

1   Chapter 1, Sophia and Caroline
15   Chapter 2, Anya and Miguel
23   Chapter 3, National News
29   Chapter 4, Volunteer
33   Chapter 5, Training
41   Chapter 6, Detention Center
47   Chapter 7, Ellen and Anthony
57   Chapter 8, Daniella and Roberto
63   Chapter 9, Elena and Matteo
69   Chapter 10, Research
75   Chapter 11, Ana and Gabriella
85   Chapter 12, Marie and Victoria
93   Chapter 13, Home
97   Chapter 14, Release
105   Chapter 15, Counsel
100   Chapter 16, Visit
115   Chapter 17, Children
123   Chapter 18, A Year Later
131   Chapter 19, Another Year Later
135   Chapter 20, A Beacon of Hope and Safety

139   *Epilogue*
140   *Acknowledgements*
141   *Notes*

To the real Sophia. The joy and love that you find in life despite so much hardship is an inspiration and gift to the world.

"Today the world is witness to a global refugee crisis of proportions not seen since World War II. But while most of the international media attention is on the refugees arriving in Europe—from countries such as Syria, Iraq, and Afghanistan—there is another protection crisis unfolding in Central America. Tens of thousands of women—travelling alone or together with their children or other family members—are fleeing a surging tide of violence in El Salvador, Honduras, Guatemala, and parts of Mexico."[1]

Prologue

Immigration has been a perennial issue in American political debate. While every country has a right to control its borders, the United States, like many other countries, has laws in place that permit the vulnerable and persecuted to request protection. The tension between who to let in—and who to keep out—creates significant conflict in the United States.

This book is about the immigration crisis at the U.S. southern border—one of the most visible places in the immigration debate. It begins in 2018 just after the Trump administration implemented several high-profile policies, including family separation, which brought immigration to the forefront of American thought. But the immigration crisis transcends presidential administrations. It will continue to remain a constant national issue into the foreseeable future—sometimes slowly simmering in the background, and sometimes a raging boil consuming public attention

In fiscal year 2019, which ran from October 2018 to September 2019, there were just shy of one million apprehensions at the U.S.-Mexico border, averaging about 80,000 people a month. This was about *double* the apprehensions the previous year.[2] The vast majority of those apprehended, about 71 percent, came from the Central American countries of El Salvador, Guatemala and Honduras—the three countries also known collectively as the "Northern Triangle." And most of them, nearly half a million people, were families.[3]

While fiscal year 2020 saw a dip in apprehension due to COVID-19, fiscal year 2021 is shaping up to be a return to previous highs, with averages of just over 70,000 apprehensions a month in the first half of the fiscal year.[4] In fiscal year 2021, the U.S. government expects more than 290,000 asylum claims from people already in the U.S.[5] The majority of those claims will be denied.[6]

While much is discussed about what happens once the families arrive and are detained, the media rarely pursues two critical questions: *who* are these families and *why* are they coming?

This books seek to address these two questions, at least in part, by telling the stories of seven families who came to the United States at the southern border and were detained by the U.S. government. I met these women and children while volunteering at a U.S. government family detention center in South Texas. They were all looking to request asylum. Each family came to the United States either by the "bridge," which is a legal port of entry from Mexico to the United States, or by the "river," that is, by crossing into the United States across the Rio Grande River that separates the U.S. southern border from Mexico.

While the families were in the detention facility, I helped prepare them for their "credible fear" interview. This meeting provides detained individuals with the opportunity to tell their story to an asylum officer, who determines whether they have a "significant possibility" of establishing the basis for asylum and therefore can be released into the United States to pursue their asylum claim.[7] If the asylum officer cannot make this finding, then detained individuals are deported back to their home countries. Some of the families discussed in this book were permitted to leave the facility and pursue their claims in the United States. Others were sent home.

After I left the detention facility, I tried to connect released families to the media so they could tell their stories to help people in the United States better understand what was driving so many families to our borders. But given the political controversies surrounding immigration, the dangers at home, and the pendency of their asylum claims, many families did not feel comfortable speaking publicly about why they came to the United States. To be clear, it wasn't that they did not want to be *heard*, it was that they did not want to be *known*.

I undertook to write this book so that their stories could be heard. I relay the stories to the reader generally as they were relayed to me, but I did change information unique to the individuals that could reveal their identity (e.g., names, countries, ages, and other identifiable aspects of their stories, etc.) or certain factual details so that no one story is directly attributable to a specific person or family.

While each family has a different story, I found that the types of threats and harms they experienced were not unique among the detained families in the detention facility. I selected seven families for this book, but met with several dozen, and with my colleagues the number rose to several hundred people during the time we were volunteering. Based on our experiences, and in talking with the legal aid staff, these seven stories were typical.

The families discussed in this book were selected to be broadly illustrative of many families detained at the border. *Who* are they? Families from Central America. *Why* are they coming? To try to survive.

Chapter 1   Sophia and Caroline

Sophia was standing in her parents' kitchen making dinner when she heard a muffled noise from somewhere inside the house. Startled, she stopped to listen, her hand resting inside the drinking glass she was using to grind avocados in a mixing bowl.

She was alone in the small house in a small village in Guatemala. Her father and brothers were at work, and her mother was with Sophia's daughter Caroline at the market.

Did they just return home from the market?—no, it did not feel like that. Her mother would have called out as they opened the door, and there would be a rush of energy as the two of them swept into the house, her mom carrying the vegetables for dinner and stories of neighborhood gossip, while little Caroline would have jumped into her mother's arms and showed her the wildflowers she picked from the side of the dirt road on the way home.

Instead, the only sound Sophia heard was the sizzling of tortillas in the frying pan. The hair stood up on the back of her neck, and she slowly turned around. The room looked—but did not feel— empty.

Sophia's instinct told her something was wrong, and her mind raced to evaluate her options: to hide, flee, or fight.

Then, she heard quiet but heavy footsteps approach from behind.

She realized the first two options were gone. She would need to fight.

Her eyes darted to the table, looking for the knife she had used to cut the avocados. She slowly reached for it.

But he reached her more quickly.

The man slammed into Sophia from behind, knocking her to the ground. The side of her face smashed into the counter as she fell. Her head seared with pain. The knife crashed uselessly to the floor, skidding under the kitchen table.

Sophia tried to throw her attacker off, but he was too strong. He pulled her ponytail, quickly yanking her head back, and then smashed her face down onto the floor before crashing down on top of her. Blood blurred her eyesight as she gasped to catch her breath. The fall had knocked the wind out of her and the weight of the man's body prevented her from catching her breath. He pressed his knees in between her shoulder blades, pinning her arms underneath her.

Sophia felt something press against her face. She noted a slightly sweet chemical smell before she lost consciousness.

When she awoke, Sophia was in a small room with concrete block walls. There was a tiny window in the back of the room far above her head and a locked metal door on one side of the room. There was no way out. Sophie had no idea where she was, or how long she had been there.

Eventually the metal door opened. Standing in the doorway was a man she used to know but had not seen in a very long time. A few years back, Sophia had moved to the city and started a job at a local bank. This man had worked with her there. He had been romantically interested in Sophia, and while she was flattered by the attention at first, she discovered from co-workers that this man was embezzling money from the bank and funneling it to gangs that had been infiltrating the city. She rejected his pursuits. Offended, he started to threaten her and eventually became violent. After he beat her and ransacked her apartment, she became fearful of what else he would do, and worried about protecting her young daughter Caroline, Sophia moved back to her parents' house where she felt safe.

Now, that safety was shattered, as he stared at her coldly from the doorway in that concrete room.

He walked over to Sophia. "I found you," he said before twisting his body sideways and whipping the back of his hand across her face. She fell, cracking the back of her head again the concrete wall. His blows rained down again, striking her over and over. She curled into a ball to protect herself, covering her head with her arms. He kicked and punched her before picking her up and throwing her against the wall. She eventually lost consciousness.

When she awoke again, he was standing over her, smoking a cigarette.

"Good, you're awake," he said. "I wanted you to be fully aware of what I am about to do to you." He then raped her violently. She fought as hard as she could, but he quickly overpowered her. When he was done, he stood up, spat on her and left.

The man came back again and again. Sometimes he was alone, and sometimes he brought other people to rape her, either his friends or people he owed money to. Months passed.

Sometimes when she thought she could hear voices outside the window she screamed for help until she lost her voice. She banged the door so hard she broke her hand. Otherwise, she sat locked in the empty concrete room. She worried about Caroline and her family, and how they must have thought she was dead.

Sophia's hands were bloody and bruised from pounding the doors. The blood and bruises mixed with other injuries from the endless attacks. She lived through the pain of multiple nose fractures, an orbital eye fracture, broken hands, fingers, and ribs. He cut her face with a knife and stabbed her in the leg with a pair of scissors. Her eyes were often swollen shut, and deep bruises covered her face and body.

After some time, Sophia discovered she was pregnant. She was initially disgusted to think that she would be forever linked to one of these evil men, bringing a child into the world that was half him. But she was also terrified. She wondered what would happen to the baby in this prison and knew that no matter how this infant came to exist, it would still be an innocent and defenseless child in need of love and safety.

Sophia tried to hide the pregnancy, scared of what the man might do. The man did not realize her condition until she was advanced in her pregnancy. He was furious when he found out and told Sophia that he would beat the baby out of her. He attacked her viciously, leaving her entire body torn, bleeding, and bruised. But her baby held on.

Sophia grew bigger, but the men did not stop showing up in the room. No one hesitated to force themselves on her, unfazed by the fact she was imprisoned in a concrete room, that she fought and screamed at them, that she was broken and beaten, and that she was heavily pregnant.

She tried to keep her mind free, thinking of her daughter Caroline and the new baby, and the life she would create for them far away from this prison. This baby was coming one way or another unless Sophia died, and she did not plan on that happening. She kept her faith in God and knew God could not mean for this room to be their grave, so she needed to focus on how she could get free and provide a safe place for her baby.

Near the end of her pregnancy, the man told Sophia that when the baby came, he would force her to watch as he killed the newborn, making her increasingly desperate to find a way out of the room.

One day after a particularly harsh beating, Sophia went into labor. It was a prolonged and painful experience that lasted several days without the baby coming.

The man eventually took her to the hospital, dropping her off but leaving a guard to stay with her. Before he left, Sophia saw the man talking to the medical staff, then he walked out the door without looking at her.

The medical staff saw that Sophia had been severely beaten and had several broken or mending bones, but said nothing. They also saw the armed guard outside her hospital room, but said nothing. The police officer at the front door of the hospital said nothing.

Finally, when Sophia was being hooked up to an IV, a nurse whispered to her, asking about her relationship to this man. Sophia explained he had kidnapped and imprisoned her, repeatedly raped her and let others do the same. She eventually fell pregnant while imprisoned, and said that the man intended to take her back to the prison when she was done where he'd murder the baby.

The nurse listened and nodded. She said that the man had threatened to kill the medical staff if they called the police. She said the officer at the front door to the hospital was corrupt. The nurse also whispered that calling the local police would not have helped anyway because most of the police worked with this man. He either paid them or threatened them.

Sophia begged the nurse for help. The nurse promised she would help as much as she could. She explained that she was going to give Sophia some medicine in case she had any infections from her assaults then treated and bandaged Sophia's recent injuries. She also said that she would try to think of a way to sneak Sophia out of the hospital after the baby was born.

She warned Sophia that they would likely need to do a Cesarean section to deliver the baby, which would make it very hard for her to escape. The surgery would cut through Sophia's abdominal muscles and into her uterus to remove the baby and would significantly inhibit her ability to move after surgery. But it might also be her only window of escape. They would try to adjust her medicines so she could walk again as soon as possible after surgery, but it was risky, and Sophia might hemorrhage and die. Without hesitating, Sophia agreed to the plan.

The nurse followed through as promised.

In the post-operating room after the Cesarean section, the nurse continued to check in with Sophia to see if she could feel her feet and move her legs. She also loaded up her IV with some medicine, squeezing the bag so it flowed faster into Sophia's bloodstream. Sophia could not move for some time, but eventually the nurse came back in to check on her and Sophia could wiggle her toes.

"I am going to give you a few more minutes," the nurse said. "Then I'll remove your catheter, load you up with pads to catch the bleeding, help you put on real clothes, and then wheel your gurney out of the room, covering you with a blanket."

"I will tell the guard that I am taking you down to breastfeed the baby in the nursery and that he can stay here if he is bothered by the sounds of babies crying. I am going to hand you your baby and wheel you out to the loading dock in the back," she continued, as she moved quickly to remove Sophia's various tubes, check and change her dressing, and gather supplies.

"It's up to you to take it from there," she said. "Do not run. Do not climb hills or stairs. Keep your incision dry and clean. Do not lift anything other than this baby. If you do, your stiches will burst, and you will hemorrhage. You cannot die, this baby needs you. Do you understand me?"

"Yes," Sophia said. "Thank you."

"There's a bus stop outside the hospital. The best thing would be for you to get on the first bus you can and get out of here."

Sophia nodded. The nurse wheeled Sophia out of the room, past the guard who eagerly stayed behind, and to the nursery to pick up the baby.

"One last question," the nurse said, as she wheeled Sophia and the baby toward a back exit of the hospital. "What did you name your baby girl?"

Sophie smiled and replied, "Her name is Maria."

"God protect Maria, God's little angel," the nurse said, reaching out to touch the baby's head in blessing. "May God bless her, and may God bless you."

Sophia fled the hospital and got on the bus. She did not have money but begged the bus driver to let her on anyway, explaining that she was trying to protect her newborn baby's life. As proof, she showed the driver her freshly stitched C-section incision. He let her on the bus.

Shortly after she boarded, the bus was flagged down and stopped by armed men. The driver told Sophia to hide under the seat with her newborn Maria. The baby continued to sleep, unfazed by the danger. The armed men boarded and searched the bus but did not find them. The bus driver continued his route, which included Sophia's hometown.

When Sophia arrived back in her town, she went to her family's house with the new baby in her arms. Her family was shocked to see her after all this time. She had vanished more than a year ago and now she stood in their home alive, battered, bruised, and holding a newborn baby.

Caroline was thrilled to see her mother. She clung to Sophia and would not leave her side.

Sophia's mother explained that they had come home to a trashed kitchen the day she had disappeared. The food was burning on the stove and there was blood on the floor next to a kitchen knife.

Her father had gone to the police begging them to search for her, but the police would not help. He wrote government officials pleading for their help, but the government would not help.

Her brothers searched for her. There were no leads as to where she might be or whether she was alive. She had just disappeared into thin air.

Sitting around the kitchen table with them after so much time, Sophia noted how exhausted her family looked. Her parents' hair had turned gray and their faces looked tired and worn. Her brothers looked far older than their years too. Sophia learned that they had each been kidnapped, beaten, and tortured while she was gone. She realized it was by the same man and his gang that had kidnapped Sophia. The family had to pay ransoms for their release. They had no money, so they needed to borrow it from neighbors. Sophia noted the scars on her brothers' arms as they talked. Her father had also been beaten several times on his walk home from work.

Sophia reached out to government for help, but no one would avail. When she went to the police, they would not write out a report. When she went to the federal government agency set up to protect abused women, they would not take her case and said they could do nothing to help.

When she went to the local prosecutor, he told her that this man's gang was powerful and particularly ruthless, and also controlled his office. The prosecutor explained that this man threatened to kill the prosecutor's young son if a case was ever brought against the gang. While sympathetic, the prosecutor would not be able to help Sophia, but he did provide her with some advice. "If he wants to find you, he'll find you," he said. "He controls the roads, he controls the buses, he controls the police, and he controls me. I recommend you lay low and hope he forgets about you. Better yet, try to disappear."

Sophia wished the man would forget about her. She had nowhere left to go for help, and she had two little children, Caroline and Maria, that depended on her. She stayed in the house and did not leave for months.

Eventually Sophia realized that the financial stress of supporting her and the children was becoming too much for her parents. An elderly neighbor offered to hire Sophia to assist with odd jobs around the house, and Sophia would only need to walk outside for a few minutes a day, a couple times a week, to get to the woman's house.

A few months after starting her new job, the man found her. Sophia was walking to work one morning when he came up from behind and attacked her, raping her in broad daylight on the road.

When Sophia had not shown up to work, her elderly neighbor had gone looking for her. She found Sophia alone and bloody in the road and helped her home. She told Sophia she was there if Sophia ever needed help. They had become close over the past few months, and the neighbor knew of Sophia's escape from her kidnappers.

When Sophia arrived home, Caroline was in school and Sophia's father and brothers were at work. Only her mother and Maria, who was bedridden with pneumonia, were at home. Her mother helped clean her injuries. They did not call the police, by now they knew it was pointless.

After Sophia was cleaned up and her new injuries bandaged, she sat at Maria's bedside, holding the baby's small hand and watching the labored rise and fall of her chest as she struggled to breath. Because Maria had been born early and experienced a traumatic birth, she often suffered from breathing issues. She had asthma and developed respiratory infections easily. Sophia sat with Maria until Caroline came home from school. The child had pneumonia.

Not all her neighbors were as supportive as Sophia's elderly friend. A few days later, some of these neighbors knocked on her parents' door. News of her attack had spread across the small community. They said the community had decided that Sophia needed to leave town because her presence brought danger to their neighborhood.

Sophia had grown up in this town and was saddened to be asked to leave, although not shocked. But Sophia and the girls had nowhere to go. This man had found her multiple times, she had no money, and the government would do nothing to stop him or to protect Sophia and her family.

The neighbors said they would lend Sophia the money to leave because they wanted her gone as quickly as possible. Sophia agreed that she likely needed to leave. Sophia would borrow the money and try to find a safe location where she could move with the girls. This would add to the mounting debt that her family already owned, but she saw no alternative.

The family began to make plans, but Sophia could not leave until Maria recovered from her pneumonia. Caroline did not know yet that they would be leaving and kept her usual routine, including going to school. Caroline had been through so much pain in her short life and the family worked hard to protect her as much as they could from the violence that engulfed the rest of the family.

But one day, the violence finally found Caroline.

Caroline was sitting in school one afternoon when Sophia's kidnapper burst through the classroom doors. The children screamed and tried to hide. The man walked up to seven-year-old Caroline and pressed a pistol into the center of her forehead.

"You're coming with me," he said.

"No," Caroline said firmly, looking up at him defiantly.

The man pointed the pistol at her teacher. "You will come with me now, or I will shoot your teacher."

At that point and having heard the children's screams, the school principal and several teachers came running into the room. The children started fleeing through the open door. In the chaos, Caroline shoved the gunman. He fled.

Caroline ran home and told her family what had happened. Sophia and her parents spent a few minutes talking. They decided Sophia and Caroline needed to leave immediately. Maria was too sick to travel, and the parents feared they would not all survive hiding, so they took Maria and escaped to a cousin's house to hide temporarily.

Sophia quickly stuffed a backpack, grabbed Caroline's hand and fled to the elderly neighbor's house to see if there was any way she could help.

The elderly neighbor called her son, Pedro, who lived in the United States. When Pedro learned Sophia's story he was appalled. A native Guatemalan who had emigrated to the United States years ago, he was familiar with the horrible things the gang was doing to families. Even still, Sophia's story shocked him.

"This woman and her little girl will die," he told his mother. "Send them to the United States so they can request asylum. They can live with me. We'll figure things out when they get here. God will help us."

Coyotes took Sophia and Caroline from Guatemala to the United States. Coyotes are human traffickers that charge thousands of dollars for the dangerous trip into the United States. Sophia and Caroline made that precarious journey from Guatemala, up to Mexico and across the Rio Grande River, which separates Mexico from the United States. They crossed on a rickety raft crowded with people in the pitch darkness of night. Once they landed on shore in the United States, the coyotes robbed them—taking their money, food, water, and phone—and told them to start walking into the cold desert night.

Sophia and Caroline walked for a couple days in the southern United States desert with no food or water, and no shelter from the searing sun and heat, or jackets for the cold nights. They did not see another soul. Caroline became weak from dehydration, and at one-point Caroline collapsed in the desert and could not walk any longer.

Sophia believed they were going to die. But she spotted and flagged down United States Customs and Border Protection patrol agents. She was so relieved to see them that she wept. The agents gave them cookies and water and were kind to them.

Sophia and Caroline were processed and ultimately sent to a U.S. government family detention center in Southern Texas.

A few days later, while serving as a volunteer attorney, I called their names in the legal aid clinic at the detention center to help prepare them for the interview that would determine if they could request asylum, or be sent back home. One misstep in the process and they would be sent home, no further questions asked. I had no prior experience in immigration, I am an energy lawyer, but the need for attorneys was so overwhelming that the legal aid clinic would take anyone with legal experience willing to help.

Sophia and Caroline were my last family on that day. As they sat across from me, with Sophia explaining what had happened to them, I thought of my own family—my children were close in age to Caroline and Maria. We were both mothers, with two children, who wanted to keep them safe and healthy, and provide them with a good life. Our children were likely learning the same things in school, and playing the same games at home, enjoying time with their siblings, and mom and extended family. We were both seeing our babies learn to walk and their older siblings learn to read, and we were both amazed at how quickly they grew and how fast they learned. But the stark difference between us right then as we sat across the table in the detention facility, was that this was a life that I could continue to live, and theirs was one that they could not.

If they were released from detention, Sophia and Caroline would go to live with Pedro, their sponsor in the United States and a person they had never met, in an unfamiliar country with an unfamiliar language. They would not likely see Maria and the rest of their family again for years—and maybe never—and rather than struggling to escape violence, they would struggle to keep their family intact while starting life over again.

I asked Sophia where Pedro lived. She could not recall the name of the town, so I pulled up a map of the United States on my computer. I turned my computer screen to face her.

After studying the map, she pointed to a city thousands of miles away from the detention center but just miles from my hometown.

Unlike the long line of other women and children I met at the detention facility, all of whom had tragic stories that led them to risk their own lives and those of their children in crossing the border, it occurred to me as I looked at the map that I could help Sophia and Caroline if they were released.

A voice called out that legal aid was closing, and all the detained women and children began to line up at the door to leave. I quickly dug in my bag for my business card and jotted my cell phone number on the back. Handing the card to Sophia, I explained, "When you are released from here, call me. Please make sure you call me." I looked her in the eyes, hoping she could understand me, and firmly pressed the card into her hand. "Please."

Her eyes met mine and she nodded her head, before turning to walk out of the room, holding Caroline's hand.

Sophia and Caroline were among dozens of people sitting in the waiting room when I called her name. If my previous interview had lasted longer, if I had taken a minute to catch up on paperwork or got up to stretch my legs or get a cup of coffee, our paths would not have crossed. But they did, and it ultimately changed both our lives.

After our meeting ended, I wrote in my intake notebook: "Sophia, 32 and Caroline, seven, were brought by coyotes into the United States. They were stopped by U.S. Customs and Border Patrol in the Texas desert. They were from Guatemala. They came by the river."

Chapter 2   Anya and Miguel

"Do you know who killed your husband?" I asked.

Anya looked down at her hands, wrung together tightly in her lap, and nodded. Then she quietly began to cry as she spoke, silent tears dripping down her cheeks and off her chin.

Four weeks before, Anya's husband was executed because he had witnessed a gang killing of a local politician. The execution occurred on a road near their rural house. Anya's husband had been walking with their five-year-old son Miguel, down to the river to fish, when they happened upon the men just as they were shooting their victim. After the father and son saw the murder, they immediately returned home. Anya's husband told her what they saw, but no one else.

The next day her husband was shot in a field near where they lived.

Anya paused before continuing, looking up. "They came for my husband, and then they came for Miguel," she said, looking at me with a wet face that was now red and blotchy from crying.

About an hour before, my partner Jason had walked out into the common area at the detention facility in south Texas and called Anya's "A" number, a government issued immigrant identification number.

"A3148ZY82," Jason called out.

A woman stood up. She was a petite, middle-aged woman, with straight hair falling just below her shoulders. Like the other women in the detention facility, she was clutching a manila envelope to her chest. It held their essential paperwork. Everything else she had with her when she was detained—if anything—would have been taken when she arrived at the facility.

When Jason called her number, she stood up waving her hand slightly in the air to let us know who she was, and then she turned and reached back for the hand of a little boy sitting with her.

"Hello, Anya," Jason said in Spanish, walking over to them. Anya shook his outstretched hand. She introduced her son Miguel, and we led them into a small meeting room. Miguel climbed into his mom's lap, as Jason dove into our now standard instructions.

He explained that we were volunteer attorneys at the detention facility here to help them prepare for their asylum "credible fear" interview, where an asylum officer would interview them to determine whether they had a credible fear of persecution or torture if they were returned to their country of origin. The asylum officer was trying to determine if there was a "significant possibility" that they would be able to establish eligibility for asylum if permitted to pursue their asylum request.[8] If they passed the interview, they would be released from detention and referred to immigration court to proceed with the asylum application process. If they did not pass, they would be sent home.

As Jason talked, I opened my computer. In the blank space at the top of the screen I entered Anya's A number.

Jason asked Anya if had come by the bridge or by the river, the two means by which nearly all families in this detention facility arrived in the United States—by the bridge, where they presented themselves at a United States' port of entry; or by the river, where they crossed into the United States across the Rio Grande River, and were then detained by U.S. Border Patrol.

We then asked Anya for some background information. When we asked Anya her age, she said she was 42.

I was surprised because she looked much older. She was just slightly older than me. Anya spoke quietly, looking at the ground when she talked. She tended to provide short responses, so we had to ask her more questions than our other clients to understand why she was here.

Eventually we pieced together her story. Anya explained that she and her husband had been field hands in a rural area of Honduras. They had five children, with Miguel their youngest. They lived in a cabin on her employer's farm in a remote area of the country.

Anya was home with Miguel when her husband was killed. They were outside picking vegetables from the garden when a neighbor came speeding down the driveway in his beat-up old truck. She knew immediately something was terribly wrong. The neighbor pulled up to the garden and said men just shot her husband and they were coming for Miguel now. He yelled for her to get in the truck.

Anya did not have time to think—she picked up Miguel and threw him in the passenger's seat while she jumped on top to cover him. Through the trees she could see a white pickup truck driving down the road leading to the farm where she lived, with masked men holding guns, sitting in the back. She ducked down to hide.

Her neighbor drove out a back road in the opposite direction, and then continued to drive the two out of town. Anya asked him to tell her other children to take care of each other. Her oldest son was in his twenties and married, and he would need to take in his younger sisters, who were 10, 13, and 15.

The neighbor dropped Anya and Miguel off at her brother's house, where they hid for a few days before making their way north. Anya explained that they intended to stay in Mexico, but when they arrived there, they were kidnapped twice.

The first time they were held for a few days in a warehouse and released. The second time they were held for several days in what looked like a garage, and then they were thrown into a river. The kidnappers pointed to the opposite shore and said, "There's America. Swim or drown."

They swam.

Anya explained to use that they were getting tired as they swam across the river and she was afraid they would drown, but she helped keep Miguel's head above water and they eventually made it across. Miguel's father had taught him how to swim when he was younger, and he was an unusually strong swimmer given his young age. She thanked God that her husband had insisted upon Miguel learning, despite Anya's concern that he was too young. God must have known it would save his life one day, she explained.

Once on shore Anya flagged down United States Customs and Border Protection and requested asylum. Anya and Miguel were soaking wet and taken to the "ice box," a cramped holding cell in a Customs and Border Protection facility. Asylum seekers called this the *hielera*, literally translated to "ice box" because of how frigidly cold they are always maintained. They spent several nights crowded into a tiny concrete room wrapped in foil blankets, before being sent to the detention center.

I watched Anya's face as she spoke, trying to process everything she was saying. Her expression did not change as she talked. She held Miguel in her lap, and he tucked his chin underneath her chin, peering out warily at us.

Anya had just described her husband's recent murder; the attempted murder of the little boy nestled in her lap; leaving four of her five children behind; and having her children lose their father, and effectively their mother and brother all in the same day.

She had described fleeing to a foreign country, being kidnapped—twice—almost drowning, then being put in cages in the United States before ending up in the detention facility in Texas, sitting in a small room talking to me.

It was no wonder she looked worn, her shoulders and neck slumped as she spoke, her eyes frequently cast downward.

It was the first time she said her story out loud to anyone.

"I know these men," Anya explained when I asked who they were.

"We are a small community. I grew up with them. My husband grew up with them. His cousin is one of them. It is because of his cousin that they always left us alone. But even that could not help us in the end." She sighed. "Our community has been plagued by evil for decades: the Devil just takes a different form, but he never goes away."

I would come to hear a lot of references to God and the Devil in speaking with the families in the detention center: about an epic battle between good and evil raging below our border and an unwavering faith in God, because without God, there would be no hope that there was a way out of this suffering.

Anya explained that the gang started out good, as vigilantes,[9] saviors dedicated to rooting out gangs and corruption in their community. The vigilantes were made up of local men tired of being victimized. They banded together, and at first set up watches to keep tabs on the gang, then they started to protect businesses against them, prevent gang-related kidnappings and extortions, and finally, they started to actively pursue and root out the group.

Frustrated at the government's corruption and ineffectiveness, the vigilantes took justice into their own hands. But the power got to their heads. They started to execute gang members, and then suspected gang members. Eventually, they started to execute other people too, such as a neighbor whose land they wanted. In fact, they started to intimidate and harass the people who they said they were protecting. Eventually, any line between the vigilantes and criminals disappeared and they replaced the gang they had effectively removed.

Anya explained that the United States, working with police from Honduras, came to her community about a year ago to help root out the gang. She said they arrested about a dozen people but missed the leader who had been forewarned by corrupt local police.

The gang continued operating as if nothing had happened, but they were crueler to the community because they believed someone among them had helped the United States. They started thinking everyone was an informant—or could be an informant. Anya believed this is why they killed her husband and wanted to kill Miguel. Not only did the gang want to eliminate witnesses, they also wanted to send a strong message to be quiet, or be killed.

Anya explained that the gang leader was a United States citizen. After the raid, he moved back to the United States, but still controlled the gang from there.

"Wait," I interrupted, surprised. "The gang leader is in the United States? Do you know where?"

Anya looked at me startled at the interruption. "Yes," she replied. "I don't know where he is, but I have his cell phone number. It's a U.S. phone number. I have it saved in my phone, which is locked up somewhere in here with the rest of my things." She motioned around her, meaning within the detention facility.

"Why do you have his number?" I asked.

She sighed. "This man had a baby with my niece," Anya explained. "He gave my niece the number in case she needed to reach him to discuss the baby. My niece gave it to me when I was in hiding after my husband was killed. She thought I might be able to explain what happened and have his men stop hunting down my son. But she is young and doesn't understand that bad men cannot be reasoned with and they certainly can't be trusted for mercy."

"Is she in a relationship with him?" I asked.

"No," Anya replied. "She never was. Like all bad men, if he sees something he wants, he takes it. That's what he did to my niece. She's pretty, but she's just a child, still a teenager."

I leaned in toward Jason who had been translating our discussion. I turned my face away from Anya and said quietly, "I think we should see if we could share this information with the government, but we would need to know this family would be kept safe."

Jason paused and looked at me. "Do you think that could harm Anya and Miguel?" he said, with a concerned look on his face.

I shrugged. "I have no idea how any of this works. If Anya shares this information, it won't be hard for people back home to figure out the information came from her. Even if she's still in the United States, she has four kids still back in Honduras that we need to think about."

"This sounds really risky. And I wouldn't even know *how* to have these discussions with the government," Jason said.

I paused and thought for a minute. "I know who to talk to about this."

I picked up the office phone and called my friend Tom, who was in the intelligence community.

When Tom found out I was calling from the detention facility, he immediately asked me to step outside and call him back from my cell phone. He explained that he was afraid the government could be listening in on our call from inside the facility. I walked out to the parking lot to get my phone and called Tom from the car.

I explained that I was in Texas working with a detained immigrant family, and that they might have information about a fugitive in the United States. He was a U.S. citizen who had been missed in a recent United States government-led raid on his gang in Honduras.

Tom asked me questions about the gang and location of the raid. I answered the questions as best I could, stressing that the family was now being targeted because the little boy had witnessed a murder.

"Okay, I am going to verify this information," Tom said. "If it checks out, I will get you a name to contact. It will likely be a United States Marshal; they deal with fugitives in the United States. It may take me a few minutes to track this down."

"I want you to sit tight," he said. "And in the meantime, do not tell anyone what you told me. I want you to be careful. Things are different at the border than they are at home. Gangs and cartels have a strong and far reach, even on people in America. Don't trust authorities. Don't trust anybody. Keep your head low and stay safe."

He hung up the phone and texted me a few minutes later. "It checks out. Expect a call."

Minutes later, my cell phone rang. It was an unknown Texas number. "Hello?" I said.

"This is Agent Walker, United States Marshal Service. May I speak with Amy?"

Chapter 3   National News

In the late spring and early summer of 2018, immigration matters at the U.S. southern border dominated the news cycle due to a series of decisions by the U.S. government that shocked not only Americans, but people around the world.

While immigration had been on the American public's mind for quite some time, there had been an influx in immigrant families seeking asylum. And the government's response—among other things—was to separate migrant children from their families. The U.S. government also struggled to provide clean and safe facilities for these detained adults and children.

While the media focused heavily on the manner in which families arrived in the United States and what happened to them once they were here, such as family separation and the conditions of the various types of immigrant detention facilities, little coverage focused on who these families were and why they were coming into the United States.

In April, the Attorney General announced a "zero tolerance" policy, directing federal prosecutors to criminally prosecute all adult immigrants entering the country illegally.[10] It was this policy decision that led to the mass separation of families. News organizations were widely reporting on this issue, which was starting to draw increased attention around the world, but the *full* extent of the problem was still not yet widely known.[11]

On June 8, in a case against the government brought by mothers separated from their children, a U.S. District Court judge in the Southern District of California issued a decision stating that it is "brutal," "offensive," and contrary to "fair play and decency" to take children from their mothers seeking asylum. In this case, the mothers had been forcibly separated from their minor children for months before bringing a suit against the government to be reunited. The judge ruled that the separation violated the due process clause of the United States Constitution, explaining that "[t]hese allegations sufficiently describe government conduct that arbitrarily tears at the sacred bond between parent and child."[12]

On June 14, 2018, Sophia, 32, and Caroline, seven, were brought by coyotes into the United States via the Rio Grande. They were from Guatemala.

From the U.S. border they were sent to the "dog pound," a holding facility near the border-crossing processing center, where each person is detained in a three-by-three-foot area enclosed by a chain link fence. They were separated from each other. From there, the family was sent to a family detention center in Texas, one of the private, for-profit family detention centers run by private contractors for Immigrant and Customs Enforcement, also known as ICE.

On June 15, 2018, Anya, 45, and Miguel, five, entered the United States by the Rio Grande and immediately turned themselves into Customs and Border Protection. They were from Honduras.

On June 15, 2018, the United States Department of Homeland Security acknowledged that in the first six weeks of the government's family separation policy nearly 2,000 children had been separated from their families.[13]

On June 17, 2018, the Secretary of Homeland Security tweeted: "You are not breaking the law by seeking asylum at a port of entry… if you are seeking asylum for your family, there is no reason to break the law and illegally cross between ports of entry."[14]

What the Secretary's statement did not note—and which I would soon learn firsthand in the detention center—was that it had become common at that time for United States and Mexican authorities to prevent people from getting to the port of entry, that Customs and Border Protection agents were forcing asylum seekers to sit at the border for weeks, and that Customs and Border Protection agents—contrary to U.S. law—were turning asylum seekers away from the port of entry once they got there.[15] I also learned that an asylum seeker must be physically present at a U.S. port of entry or in the United States to apply for asylum, so by turning people away, people seeking asylum were unable to request it.[16]

On June 18, 2018, Ellen, 28, and Anthony, six, presented themselves at a bridge at a United States port of entry and requested asylum. They were from Honduras.

On June 18, 2018, the United Nations High Commissioner for Human Rights, the head of the United Nations Human Rights Council,[17] a 47-nation body, criticized the United States' policy of separating migrant parents from their children after they entered the United States at the Mexican border. They called it child abuse. "The thought that any state would seek to deter parents by inflicting such abuse on children is unconscionable," said Zeid Ra'ad al-Hussein, the High Commissioner.[18]

On June 19, 2018, Daniella, 36, and Roberto, seven, arrived by raft on the Rio Grande dividing the United States and Mexico, and turned themselves into a United States Customs and Border Protection patrol requesting asylum. They were from Guatemala.

Daniella and Roberto entered the United States by river after being turned away at a port of entry by U.S. Customs because, they were told, "America was full." From the border, they were sent to the "dog pound" before being led to the "ice box," a freezing, overcrowded holding cell. Finally, they too reached a family detention center in Texas.

On June 20, 2018, Elena, 41, and Matteo, 13, entered the United States by the Rio Grande River and requested asylum. They were from El Salvador. When they arrived in the United States, they were detained and ultimately sent to a family detention center, also in Texas.

In the few weeks prior, pictures had started to emerge and continued to appear daily in the media of little kids, dirty, crying, locked behind barbed-wire fences, sleeping on concrete floors, alone without their parents to protect or comfort them. Furthermore, the government was also sending children back to their countries without their parents, or parents without their children, oftentimes using this as leverage so parents would have to withdraw their asylum claims to get their children back.[19]

When it became widely known to the American public that the United States government was separating children (many of them toddlers and babies) from their families and putting them in detention, a number of law firms—including my own—stepped up to challenge the government's action, bringing additional support and resources for litigation.[20]

The United States Department of Justice was repeatedly issuing guidance for processing asylum claims that ran contrary to the laws of the United States. Such acts spurred significant outpouring of support from the legal community to challenge these policies and practices in court and provide legal assistance to families in detention. Many of these challenges were successful, but the sheer volume and ever-shifting nature of the changes made it difficult to ensure U.S. government agencies were following the law.

On June 20, 2018, my law firm sent an email to our offices across the United States. The email recognized that several attorneys and staff had expressed concern about the number of detained families seeking asylum and the current United States policy of separating families at our southern border. It noted several lawsuits that have been filed across the country challenging certain detention policies of the Department of Homeland Security.[21]

The email went on to discuss a project in Texas focused on representing detained immigrants at detention centers. It noted that several non-profit organizations had joined forces to respond to the United States government's current family detention and separation policies. The firm was evaluating whether to send teams of attorneys to Texas to provide legal support for children and mothers detained at a family detention center. The email called for volunteers to help on this project.

Within an hour, the volunteer slots were filled. I was one of them.

On June 20, 2018, in response to the national outcry, the President signed an Executive Order designed to put an end to family separation.

On June 22, 2018, Ana, 42, and Gabriella, 12, presented themselves at a U.S. port of entry bridge and requested asylum. They were from El Salvador. Ana and Gabriella had waited in line for several weeks before they were able to get to a Customs agent. The first time they presented at the U.S. border, they were told to come back another day. The next day, Mexican authorities physically blocked them and others from getting into the Customs line. Ana and Gabriella were assaulted and robbed in Mexico while they waited. After trying for two weeks, they finally reached a Customs agent and requested asylum. They were permitted into the country and detained. Once in custody in the United States, they were taken to the ice box, and then a family detention center in Texas.

On June 26, 2018, the United States District Court for Southern California, in a case brought against the government by the American Civil Liberties Union on behalf of immigrants separated from their children, issued a preliminary injunction that ordered the government to return children under five years old to their parents within 14 days, and within 30 days for children five and over.[22]

The government informed the court that an estimated 2,700 immigrant children were separated from their parents or caregivers as a result of the government's family separation policies in the two months it had been implemented, although it later admitted that this number may have been underestimated by thousands of children.[23]

Nearly half of these children were under the age of ten and nearly all were from Guatemala, Honduras, or El Salvador. Several internal government agency audits later uncovered that the initial numbers were not accurate and, during Congressional testimony, an inspector at the United States Department of Health and Human Services' Inspector General's Office testified that, "exactly how many more children were separated is unknown" because there was no system that reliably tracked separated children.[24]

On June 27, 2018, one day after the preliminary injunction was issued, Marie, 24, and Victoria, one and a half years old, entered the United States by the Rio Grande River. They had come from El Salvador. When they crossed into the United States, they were detained, sent to the ice box and then on to a family detention center in Texas.

Chapter 4   Volunteer

In early July, I received a firm email saying that nearly 30 volunteers would be heading down to Texas to volunteer at the largest family detention facility in the United States. The first group of 15 or so was told to plan on arriving in San Antonio several days later, where we would drive to southern Texas to volunteer at a U.S. government family detention center.

This detention facility was where the U.S. government sent women and children detained at the U.S. border, either at the actual border itself, or soon after crossing into the United States. Several documents were attached to the email, including a training manual and a long list of rules when in the facility issued by the private contractor that ran the detention facility.

I booked my flight to Texas. I left in five days.

I spent the bulk of the week wrapping up work projects and trying to get up to speed on immigration law. As an energy lawyer, I knew I was way outside my element, and I wanted to at least have a grasp of the basic tenets before I left. I read dozens of court cases, including the flurry of recent immigration decisions coming out of U.S. federal courts. I read news articles on the detention facilities to get a better idea of what I could expect, and poured over primers on asylum law.

I also participated in a volunteer planning call. I took it from my bedroom while my husband played with the kids in the yard.

During the call, I learned that our team would be volunteering with a group of non-profits providing legal aid at the family detention center. A couple years earlier, when the Department of Homeland Security's Immigration and Customs Enforcement, or "ICE," started to significantly expand its family detention facilities, several groups joined forces to provide legal services to detained immigrants.

The non-profit groups provided and coordinated pro bono legal support at some of the biggest detention centers, but the demand far outstripped their capacity, oftentimes leaving one lawyer to support thousands of detained families. It was like a medical clinic in war. Triage was quick and the goal was to just prevent the worst things from happening to the highest number of people. There was no time or resources for much more.

At the detention facility where our team would be heading, volunteers worked in weekly shifts to represent families before handing off pending cases to the next batch of volunteers. We would spend Sunday evening in training and be in the facility first thing Monday morning to begin work.

At the end of the call, we were asked to explain why we had volunteered. A few volunteers explained that they became interested in heading to the border to help families stay together and to help women and children get out of jail while their asylum cases were being processed.

"I am coming to volunteer," I said, "because I have two young children. I would do anything in the world to protect them, and I imagine these women are doing the same for their children, so I want to try to help them."

Then one man spoke up. "I am coming to the detention facility because I am Jewish," he said.

"In June 1939, the German ocean liner St. Louis and its 937 passengers, almost all Jewish, were turned away from the port of Miami, forcing the ship to return to Europe, where many of the passengers died in the Holocaust.[25] As a Jew, who lost my grandparents in the Holocaust, I cannot sit back and watch people fleeing death turned back from the United States because of fear, ignorance, and bigotry."

Two more people said that they had volunteered because they were also Jewish and wanted to protect people trying to escape harm.

Another person spoke up. "I am coming to the detention facility because I was a refugee who immigrated to the United States. I lived in a refugee camp when I was three and four, before we were able to come to the United States. People helped my family when we arrived here with absolutely nothing, and now it is my turn to pay it forward."

Another person offered that they had volunteered because they had also come to the United States as a refugee during childhood.

My husband come back into the house and put the kids to bed as the call was wrapping up. I went upstairs and looked in on the kids sleeping in their beds. Side by side, with beautiful round faces lightly dotted with newfound summer freckles. I kissed them both on their foreheads, thanking God for our blessings.

Chapter 5   Training

The night we arrived in Texas the volunteers assembled for a training organized by the legal aid clinic that worked at the detention facility. Training was in a small conference room, filled with two rows of folding tables, with two people to a table for the length of the room.

The attorney who ran the legal aid clinic was a young woman named Lillian. Lillian had a warm smile and an open demeanor which made her approachable to the volunteers. She was also intelligent and well-spoken. I learned she was well-respected, not only by the detained women and children she represented, but also by the detention facility staff.

Lillian began the meeting by introducing herself and the other legal aid staff, which consisted of a few paralegals and interns. She also introduced a couple serial volunteer attorneys. They had volunteered so many times at the clinic that they were identified as initial resources for information when we were at the clinic.

After introductions, Lillian asked who spoke Spanish. Nearly everyone in the room raised their hand. I was among the few people who didn't.

Lillian started the training.

First, she went over the rules of the detention center. Lillian stressed that we must follow the rules. If we did not, we would be asked to leave by the detention facility staff and not be allowed to return to the facility. More importantly, we might jeopardize the legal aid group's continued pro bono legal services at the detention facility.

There were a lot of rules. Among others, we could not bring our phones into the facility, but we could bring our computers and hot spots.

We could start as early as seven o'clock in the morning but needed to be out of the facility by five o'clock in the evening every day.

We could not share any food or water with the "residents" of the detention facility, that is, the detained women and children. The tap water at the facility, like that in the rest of town, was contaminated and would make people sick if consumed.

While we could shake hands, we could not hug the "residents." If the detention facility staff saw us hugging someone, we would be kicked out.

Our clients were the "residents" at the detention center who had asked for legal aid. These were women and children who had requested asylum and been detained by Customs and Border Protection. Use of legal aid services was voluntary for the detained women and children at the facility.

We were going to be providing legal support in several capacities. Most of us would be helping clients prepare for their credible fear interviews. Some of us would also work on family separation and reunification matters.

Lillian explained that immigrants at the detention center generally entered the United States by one of two ways: a port of entry, which the legal aid team called "by the bridge," or not through a port of entry, which they called "by the river." These two distinctions were made because most clients either came by a legal port of entry into the United States at a bridge going over the Rio Grande River, or came directly into the United States by crossing the river illegally on a raft or sometimes by swimming.

People apprehended after crossing the border illegally could still apply for asylum, but the application is automatically opposed by the government and applicants endure a more adversarial, court-like hearing on the asylum application. This is known as defensive asylum.

Someone asked why asylum seekers would cross by the river when they could just come to a port of entry. Lillian explained there could be a number of reasons for this, including that many people had hired coyotes who took them by the river; others might not know the legal difference between requesting asylum at the bridge or after crossing the river; while others heard that the United States and Mexican authorities make it difficult for people to come to a port of entry and request asylum, so they get scared away. In fact, Mexican immigration officials often physically block asylum seekers from approaching United States border posts.

It was not uncommon at the time for Customs and Border Protection officers to reject asylum seekers at ports of entry—which the law prohibits them from doing. They have been known either to turn them away, telling them to come back another time, or to tell them that America was full and they couldn't apply for asylum. Customs and Border Protection would also restrict the number of people who could seek asylum each day, sometimes limiting it to one or two families, leaving the other families to wait in line in Mexico for weeks in dangerous conditions. This policy also left these families vulnerable to the gangs in Mexico, who often kidnap people to extort ransoms from their families in the United States or back home.[26] As a result, immigrants often come by the river.[27]

If immigrants came one of these ways, by the bridge or by the river, without the proper travel documents, and entered the United States, they would usually be ordered removed by the Department of Homeland Security. The removal order usually occurs quickly, especially if they came by the river. However, if they express a fear of returning to their home country, they are generally sent to a detention center, where they would be interviewed by an asylum officer. The asylum officer is a Department of Homeland Security employee responsible for determining whether an immigrant might establish eligibility for asylum, withholding of removal, or deferral of removal under the Convention Against Torture. If so, they would be able to remain in the United States while their application is pending.

For detained immigrants seeking asylum at the detention center, Lillian explained that the credible fear interview was critical. One of two outcomes would stem from this interview. If they did not pass the interview, the mother and her children would be deported and could not apply for asylum because they needed to be physically present in the United States to do so.

If they did pass the interview, the mother and her children could be released in the United States, usually to a sponsoring family. It gets them out of detention, and it starts them on the asylum application process.

Lillian told us to always start by asking our clients their "A" number, which is their United States government assigned immigration tracking number. The government tracks immigrants by A numbers and, as a result, this is how legal aid tracks their cases. She stressed the importance of properly tracking the women and children by their assigned numbers in the legal aid computer database, so information was not lost. The information was also helpful in searching for immigrants in ICE's detainee locator if we needed to find where someone, such as a family member, was being held elsewhere in the country.

Lillian went over the grounds for asylum. She explained that under U.S. law, asylum protection is available to immigrants who have left their country because they feared they would be harmed for belonging to certain groups of people.

She explained that there were five main elements of asylum.

First, that an individual had suffered significant "harm" in the past, which included also the *threat* of harm. The harm had to be serious, such as a threat of murder or significant physical harm, torture, rape, slavery, or forced prostitution.

Second, that an individual had a well-founded fear of future harm.

Third, that the harm was "on account of" one of five protected grounds: race, religion, political opinion, nationality, or membership in a protected social group.

Fourth, that the state of origin was unable or unwilling to protect the individual.

And, fifth, that internal relocation in-country was not reasonable.[28]

For children, the same standards apply, but the views, such as the threat of harm, would be from the perspective of a child.

We walked through dozens of court decisions interpreting each of these elements, including how different courts across the United States have handled application of these elements differently.

Lillian explained that on June 11, 2018, the Attorney General ordered United States immigration courts to stop granting asylum to victims of domestic abuse and gang violence.[29] But, a huge number of people in detention are victims of this type of violence. The ruling significantly impacted women and children from Central American countries who were fleeing horrific violence perpetrated by warring gangs.

Most asylum seekers in the detention centers were coming from El Salvador, Guatemala, and Honduras—also known as the "Northern Triangle" countries—because of extreme violence combined with governments that could not, or would not, protect them. Femicide and infanticide ran rampant in the Northern Triangle and women and children were particularly vulnerable. The murder rates in these countries were amongst the highest in the world, particularly for women. The known homicide rates for women in El Salvador, Guatemala, and Honduras rank first, third, and seventh, respectively, on the entire planet.[30]

In addition to asylum, Lillian explained that another legal framework we needed to be aware of was the United Nations Convention against Torture and Other Cruel, Inhuman or Degrading Treatment or Punishment. This is an international human rights treaty that aims to prevent torture and other acts of cruel or inhuman treatment. The Convention forbids signatory states, which includes the United States, from transporting people to any country where there is reason to believe they will be tortured.[31]

Lillian explained the unique laws related to the treatment of children. She explained that during the 1980s and 1990s, there were several lawsuits brought against the government for mistreatment of unaccompanied children. These lawsuits resulted in a 1997 legally binding settlement agreement, under which the United States government would seek to avoid holding unaccompanied children for longer than 20 days, and during detention, the children would be provided with food and water; medical assistance during emergencies; toilets and sinks; kept in rooms with adequate temperature controls and ventilation, and with adequate supervision; and permitted to remain in contact with family members they were apprehended with.[32] This became known as the "Flores Settlement" and still applies to children's detention in the United States.[33]

Our primary job as volunteer attorneys would be to talk to the women and children about what happened to them and help them tell their stories in a clear and concise manner during their very short credible fear interview with the U.S. government's asylum officer. We also helped explain the asylum process and next steps after the interview.

She explained that given the short duration of the interview, and the fact that many families had experienced extensive harm over long periods of time, that we should advise them to focus on the "first, worst, last"—that is, when were they first harmed, what was the worst thing that happened to them, and when were they last harmed.

Finally, Lillian explained that volunteers should be self-aware and mindful of signs of secondary trauma in themselves. Secondary trauma is the emotional duress that can happen when someone hears about the firsthand trauma experiences of someone else. Signs of secondary trauma include insomnia, inability to talk about our experience, and emotional volatility. We were encouraged to talk to a mental health provider, family or friends after our volunteering experience.

I thought this recommendation seemed a bit dramatic, but I also did not anticipate at the time the kind of stories people were going to tell us.

We finished the training, and Lillian told us to show up at the detention center at seven o'clock the next morning to go through security.

Chapter 6   Detention Center

We left the hotel early the next morning to head over to the detention center. Our group and the other legal aid volunteers were leaving at the same time, so we formed a caravan of cars from the hotel parking lot and made our way to the facility. It was about a 15-minute drive from the hotel.

The town had little more than 4,000 people. The only parts of town we had seen on arrival were a gas station, a Mexican food truck on the side of the road, and the hotel. We drove past each again on the way to the detention facility. We also drove past the men's federal penitentiary that was down the road from the immigrant family detention center. The two facilities were the town's largest employers. We were on the outskirts of town, so we saw no houses or businesses on the drive each morning, and the open and flat land was uninterruptedly beige, with sand punctuated by little, scrubby plants and pockets of grass bathed in sunlight.

We took a few turns and continued through the otherwise barren surroundings until we saw some structures appear in the distance. The buildings were hard to see at first because they were beige against the beige landscape, but the framing of grey barbed-wire fencing slowly brought the facility into shape as we drew closer. We passed a sign that said the name of the facility, along with the words "United States Customs and Immigration Enforcement." We then turned into an immense dirt and gravel parking lot, driving for a few minutes before pulling into a parking space in the otherwise nearly empty lot.

We had been told not to take any pictures of the facility and that cell phones were not permitted, so we left them in the car.

The facility was made up of dozens of beige trailers—the kind used at construction sites or temporary classrooms at overcrowded schools. It looked like there were big white tents behind them.

Most of the detention facility could not be seen from the parking lot, so I never had a good idea of what the whole facility looked like. It turns out that I never would, because I only went to three adjacent trailers: the security trailer, the legal aid trailer, and the trailer where they conducted credible fear interviews.

As I stepped out of the car, the sunlight on the dirt and buildings glared extraordinarily brightly, lighting up everything a glaring shade of beige. Wavy heat radiated off the ground.

After we parked, my colleague Ravi opened the trunk and we loaded our arms with bottled water.

"Nothing like carrying 100 pounds of water in 100-degree heat," he said, smiling good naturedly.

We struggled to carry in the water, food for the week, and computer bags.

Inside the first trailer was the security building. We had arrived just as the facility was opening, so there was a long security line, with employees, legal aid, and volunteers going through the security check simultaneously. It was like going through a security line at the airport, but everything needed to come out of our bags, and we had an absurd amount of water to put up on the security belt.

After we passed security, we needed to register at the front desk and present our attorney bar cards, which showed we were eligible to practice law. They held onto our bar cards at the security desk while we were in the facility. When we left, they returned them. This was a strange practice I had never seen before, even when visiting a jail.

We crossed a breezeway and entered the adjacent trailer. This was where the legal aid group worked. It was large and rectangular, with a big middle room, surrounded on the perimeter by smaller side rooms for individual client meetings. The small side offices had desks or tables with a phone and some chairs. There was a security desk at the two entrances to the building, one from the security building and one that led into the area where the residents were detained.

One of the small side rooms in the corner functioned as a breakroom of sorts, and it was filled with water and snacks for the legal team. There was nowhere to get lunch or food throughout the day, so the team relied on the snacks to stave off hunger until the end of the day. We dropped off the water and snacks that we had brought with us into that room to share with the others.

Lillian was already there running around. She said a quick hello before running off.

I looked over at Ravi. "Do you know what would be most helpful before the clients arrive?"

"The clients are going to come at nine o'clock and we can begin our credible fear prep meetings," he said. "Before they arrive, one of the legal aid staff will show us around and how we can update client documents and be helpful between clients."

"Okay, that sounds like a plan," I said.

We formed teams for the client interviews. I was paired with my colleague Jason. He spoke Spanish and Portuguese. He used to live in Central America. I was thrilled to be teamed with someone that not only spoke Spanish but was also familiar with Central America.

At nine o'clock exactly, the back of the room opened. Through the doors walked about 60 women and their children. They looked nearly identical. Their clothes had been issued by the detention facility. The women and children wore a combination of bright reds, yellows, and blues, in a combination of sweatpants, sweatshirts, t-shirts, and sneakers. They each held a single manila envelope, which contained their paperwork, but otherwise had nothing else with them.

Most of the children were under ten, many were toddlers, and some were babies. There were a lot of children. They wore the same bright colored clothes as their mothers.

We looked at them as they came in, and they looked at us, before taking a seat in a big circle of chairs in the middle of the room. They sat down with their children on their laps or on a chair next to them.

There was a "playroom" in the back of the room that blasted SpongeBob SquarePants throughout the day. I did not see any toys in the room and I never saw any children go into the room, even when they were waiting for hours with their mothers.

The children did not smile. They did not speak. They did not play. They did not wander around like kids usually do when they are in a new place. They just sat, looking dazed and scared. Many were coughing.

Nothing could prepare me for the emotional impact of seeing children in jail in the United States.

I could not stop looking at the children. Suddenly, an issue that was nothing more than words in a newspaper, and political discussions about immigration and ethics, became a room full of real mothers and real children, who were willing to uproot their entire lives to come to a country they did not know, hoping it was better than the ones they were leaving. I thought of my kids, so happy and playful, like children should be, and imagined them sitting there among these children, dressed like crayons, looking like zombies.

Jason was next to me. He was clenching his jaw, and his hands were curled into fists.

He turned to me. "Why aren't the kids moving at all? They're not talking or playing. They look catatonic. Do you think they are drugged?"

I looked at him surprised.

"Well, they're jailing kids and taking them away from their parents, so I do not know what the level is that they are *not* willing to sink to," he said.

Ravi walked by, overhearing our conversation. "This is just the first group," he said. "A new group of people will come in every couple hours until the end of the day. And the next day will be the same, and the day after that. Until we call their name, they will just sit there with their kids, for hours. The moms can put the kids in the daycare when they come to legal aid, but many of them don't want to. Many of them were separated from their kids at some point and know that the U.S. government is separating children from their parents, so they won't let their kids out of their sight now."

There was a water dispenser in the back of the room. One of the mothers went and took a small plastic cup next to the dispenser and filled it with water before handing it to a little girl, who looked to be around four.

"The kids get sick a lot, they throw up and get diarrhea." Ravi continued. "And you can hear the coughing. Many of these kids clearly have respiratory infections. It doesn't help that many of them came from overcrowded holding cells before they arrived here."

"Maybe that explains why the children are all sitting around listlessly," I said. "And I imagine many of them are in shock, too."

We paused again, watching the families get settled in.

"This isn't right," Jason said again.

He turned to me. "Listen, we need to help as many of these families as we can. We need to dig deep—from first thing in the morning until we're kicked out of here every day. We need to help as many of these families as we can."

I nodded in agreement, looking at the big group of women and children sitting in front of us.

Jason walked across the room to the list of detainees and called out the first on the list.

Chapter 7   Ellen and Anthony

"A314638RT58, Ellen," Jason called.

A woman stood up, clutching her manila envelope, and reached over to take the hand of her son, a little boy around six, a little older than my son.

"Hello, Ellen," Jason said in Spanish, reaching out to shake her hand. "My name is Jason, and this is my colleague Amy. We are both lawyers. Amy doesn't speak Spanish, so I am going to translate our conversation for her."

Ellen shook Jason's outstretched hand, and gave me a small, polite smile.

The first thing I noticed about Ellen is that she was strikingly beautiful. Ellen also appeared confident. She stood up straight, with her chin tilted up proudly.

"This is my son Anthony," she said putting her arm around him. Anthony had big brown eyes, a round cherub face, and dimples in his cheeks. He did not look quite as sad as the other kids, which made me a little relieved. Maybe this first preparation session would not be so hard.

Anthony had impeccable manners for a young child, and like his mom, he seemed to be confident.

Anthony reached out and shook Jason's hand, and then offered his hand to me, talking to me quickly in Spanish as I shook his hand.

I looked at Jason nervously. I had no idea what he was saying, but I did not want Anthony to think I was ignoring him by not responding.

Jason saw my concern and jumped in. "Amy doesn't speak Spanish," he said to Anthony in Spanish.

Anthony started to laugh and continued to speak to me.

Jason smiled and turned to me. "Anthony says of course you speak, he heard you talk. He thinks you're playing a joke on him. I don't think he realizes that you're speaking English, not Spanish."

"Anthony," I said in English, "I only speak English. I am sorry that I don't understand you, but I would like to be your friend."

When Jason translated, Anthony looked at me and cracked up. He slapped his leg and waved his finger at me as if to say, "Oh, you joker!"

He continued to speak to me rapidly in Spanish.

I had no idea why he thought this was so funny, but it made me laugh, which made Jason laugh, which made Ellen laugh.

"Well, this was a good way to start," I thought. We walked toward the meeting room. Jason went in first, and then Ellen.

Anthony reached out to hold my hand as we walked toward our room, and I instinctively reached back for his. It was a mom instinct. But then I remembered that I was not allowed to take his hand.

We were still in the middle of the room, in front of the detention center staff. If they saw me holding Anthony's hands I would get kicked out and not be allowed back into the facility. It could also jeopardize the ability of legal aid to continue to operate in the facility. As I remembered this rule, I quickly pulled my hand back before our fingers touched. Anthony looked up at me surprised.

I was frustrated that I could not speak Spanish. I wanted to tell Anthony that I would love to take his hand, but it was not allowed. I wanted to tell him that he was the same age as my son, and that I am sure if they met they would be good friends. I wanted to ask Anthony if he liked dinosaurs and baseball, like my son. I wanted to give him a chance to be a kid in this serious and scary place.

But I could not talk to him because I could not speak Spanish and he could not speak English. It made me feel mute, like I could not communicate at all. I smiled at Anthony and pointed toward the meeting room. I could not think of anything else to do that he would understand.

We walked into our meeting room and closed the door. I was glad to be in a private room. Outside in the central area I was so afraid to accidently do something I should not. I was also glad to be teamed with Jason, because at least with him, I had a voice again because he could translate for me.

"Why don't you explain who we are and why we are here, and I'll take notes and ask questions through you," I suggested to Jason. "Just give me a second to start up my computer."

I logged into the legal volunteer's data entry site. In the blank space at the top of the screen, I entered Ellen's A number.

Jason explained to Ellen that we were pro bono attorneys here to help them prepare for their asylum credible fear interview. He explained that we did not work for the government, but that we were there to help them. He explained that we were here to tell her about the United States asylum process and to explain how the credible fear interview works, and the types of questions they would ask so that she could provide clear and concise responses to the asylum officer's questions during an otherwise short interview.

Jason asked Ellen if she understood what he just said.

Ellen indicated that she understood. She sat stiffly upright in her chair, with no emotion on her face. Anthony sat patiently in the chair next to her. His legs barely reached past the edge of the seat of the chair.

Jason asked Ellen to provide some basic background information.

Ellen explained that she was from Honduras; she was 28 and married to Anthony's father. Anthony was six. Ellen and Anthony arrived at the bridge and requested asylum at United States Customs. From the border they were sent to the "dog pound" the holding facility near the border crossing processing center, for a couple days. Ellen and Anthony were separated at the dog pound, but reunited when sent to the detention center.

"Why are you afraid to return to your country?" Jason asked.

"Because Anthony will be murdered," she responded. Jason paused and looked down at the floor for a moment.

"What did she say?" I asked, leaning in toward him.

"She said Anthony would be murdered," Jason said quietly leaning in toward me. I looked at Ellen, who looked back at me, and then I looked over at Anthony sitting on his hands patiently in his chair.

"Jason, can you ask Ellen if she would like to put Anthony in the playroom while we talk so he doesn't have to hear this?"

"No," Ellen responded firmly to the question when Jason asked, reaching out and taking Anthony's hand.

"I do not want him away from me. They took him away from me at the dog pound, and I hear that other mothers do not even know where their kids are. He will stay with me. I am his mother. It is my job to protect him. That is why we came to the United States."

Jason looked over at me. "I don't blame her," I said. "I would say the exact same thing if I were in her place. Can you tell her that of course Anthony can stay with her?"

When he told her this, Ellen seemed to relax.

"Who will kill Anthony?" Jason continued.

"The gang," Ellen responded, her voice flat.

"Why does the gang want to kill Anthony?"

Ellen explained that she was a hairdresser in Honduras. She and her husband owned a salon in the center of town, in a row of other stores.

She explained that the gangs controlled the town, and that people could not leave or enter the town without their permission.

"I grew up in this town and we had no gang," she explained. "When I opened my business, we had no gang, but now we do, and they have taken over the town."

"About six months ago, several men came into my store," she continued. "One of them spoke to me and told me that I needed to start paying 'rent' to him, and that he would be by in two days to collect it. I own my business. He was from the gang, and this is how they operate—they demand extortions from business owners."[34]

Ellen and her husband talked to the other store owners, and they all decided not to pay the extortion.

The men went to the police and made a police report. The next morning when Ellen and her family arrived at the salon to open for the day, they saw police at the business next door.

They walked over to see what was going on and inside saw the bodies of the store owners, and their two children. They had been murdered.

Ellen took Anthony home while her husband stayed to talk to the police. He told the police about the gang's extortion and that they had filed a police report the day before.

The police officer at the scene looked him in the eye and coldly told him there was no police report.

Her husband went down to the police station and was told again there was no report. He was also told they would not take a new report.

Ellen explained that she grew up with the parents who had been murdered. She had gone to school with them and saw the family at church each week. They were friends and Anthony had played with their kids. She explained that Anthony had seen the dead bodies of his friends before she rushed him home.

When the gang came to their salon for the extortion the next day, Ellen and her husband paid it. Because they had gone to the police, the price had now gone up, and the gang would continue to raise the amount.

Ellen explained that the extortion became higher than the money she made at the salon, so they had to start borrowing money from family and friends to pay it. They knew what would happen if they could not pay.

Ellen could not sell the store because it was their only source of income, and no one would buy it now because of the gang extortion and murders, and she could not move because there was nowhere else to go—the gang controlled the entire town and surrounding towns and would not let them leave.

"Then one day," she said, "they came to us and raised the 'rent' again. We could not pay it. We had borrowed all we could. We did not know what to do. The day rent was due, we left our house and never returned. We went to my parents' house. My father hid us in the back of his pickup and drove us to a cousin's house across town. Anthony and I hid inside in a closet in his house. We did not move, and we did not say a word."

Ellen's husband went off with her father. "When my husband came back, he was alone," she said. "He was able to borrow enough money to pay a coyote to take me and Anthony to the United States. We needed to leave immediately. We did not even have a chance to pack anything. We had no change of clothes, I was wearing sandals, not even sneakers. We did not have any paperwork, the only document I had was Anthony's birth certificate."

"We left that night, evading the gang checkpoints that cover

Honduras, and made our way north to the United States border."

Ellen paused and looked at us.

"I did not get to say goodbye to my father, or my mother, or the rest of my family. I do not know if I'll see my husband again. I do not know if he's okay, I do not know if any of them are okay."

"I don't want to be here," Ellen said quietly. "I want to be home and I want my life back. That is where my family is. That is where my husband is. I was lucky, I had a successful business. We were not rich, but we had what we needed. We had a loving family, we could put food on the table, a roof over our head, and clothes on our back. We could take care of Anthony. I was proud of our business and our success."

"Here, I have nothing. I am treated like nothing." Ellen spoke slowly and deliberately. "But I am here because Anthony would be killed if I was home. They might kill me, and my husband, and my parents too, but I know they would kill him. He's just six years old. We cannot hide or move, there is nowhere to go. Gangs control everything. They check your ID when you get on or off a bus, when you drive into or out of town, when you even walk down the street.[35] We cannot go to another town controlled by a new gang, because they will check our ID and will assume we are spies for the old gang and kill us. It was a dangerous trip through Guatemala and Mexico to get to the United States.'

"We have a cousin in the United States. He said I could live with them in California while my asylum claim was being processed. This is the only place I could go. It is the only place where I could be away from the gangs and have a roof over my head. I have to protect my son."

I listened and looked at Anthony, who was quietly holding his mom's hand as she talked, with his eyes downcast at the floor.

We kept talking, trying to learn more about them to see if they might have been targeted for being in one of the protected groups.

After all, it was not enough for someone to want to kill you, it must be because of race, political opinion, religion, nationality or membership in a "particular social group."

If they were permitted to stay, Ellen's cousin in the United States would serve as her sponsor while she pursued her asylum claim. A sponsor for immigration purposes is a commitment by someone in the United States who accepts legal responsibility for financially supporting the sponsored immigrants.

Every family I would meet with during our time at the detention facility had a sponsor.

When we finished our meeting, we stood up to walk them out.

Anthony called me over with his finger. I thought he wanted to say something to me, so I leaned over to listen. He kissed me on my cheek.

I pulled back quickly.

Jason shook his head and said "no" when he realized Anthony was kissing my cheek. I had not realized what Anthony was going to do, and I pulled back once I did, but I am sure that one act would have been enough to get me kicked out. I looked at the door to make sure it was closed. But there was a small window in the door, and I looked around again, scared that someone would haul me out.

It felt surreal, that this little boy just sat through and listened to this horrible discussion about all the ways gangs wanted to kill him, just like they had killed his friends—young children just like him. My human instinct was to hug him, and instead I had to pull back when he unexpectedly kissed me on the cheek.

We finished walking them out and headed back into the interview room to finish up our case notes before calling the next person.

"Do you think every case is going to be like that?" I asked Jason.

"Honestly, that sucked. I hope not," Jason said. "That was really tough to listen to. And I had to go through it twice—first listening to it and then repeating it to you when I translated."

"There are so many places that failed to protect this family. And it's not going to get better," he said. "El Salvador, Guatemala, and Honduras need outside help to fight the gangs and government corruption—so the police officers who wouldn't take the police report from Anthony's father are fired, or better yet, thrown in jail. If gangs were not effectively becoming the government, then people like Ellen and Anthony, who would rather be able to stay home, would not have to flee here."

I stopped taking notes for a moment to look at Ellen and Anthony. I thought how preposterous it felt to sit in a room with a child and his mother and ask the mother to explain *why* someone wanted to murder her child. Under asylum law, it was not the fact that a child would be murdered that determined whether they qualified for asylum but rather the reason why someone wanted to murder him in the first place. Anthony needed to be targeted because he was in a protected class in order to qualify for asylum.

We finished up the meeting and Jason walked them out. I wrote in my notebook: "Ellen, 28, and Anthony, six, presented themselves at a United States port of entry and requested asylum. They were from Honduras. They came by the bridge."

Jason walked over to the list and called another name.

Chapter 8   Daniella and Roberto

"A31VY386983, Daniella," Jason called.

A woman stood up, clutching her manila envelope, and reached over to take the hand of her son, a little boy around seven. Daniella was short and round, and her son, Roberto, was short and round too. They both had warm smiles, but it was still the kind of smile you force to be polite when you meet someone new. Roberto was missing one of his top front teeth and kept wiggling another loose tooth as we talked to his mom.

Jason introduced us, and we led them into a meeting room.

I opened my laptop. In the blank space at the top of the screen I entered Daniella's A number and Jason started the meeting by asking Daniella for her background information.

Daniella explained that she was from Guatemala and worked in a factory. Her son, Roberto, was in second grade. They lived in a small village. She explained that Roberto's father, her husband, was a drunk and abusive to her. When he started to abuse Roberto a few years ago, she left him and moved back in with her parents, who also worked in the factory. She never heard from Roberto's father again. They did not have much, but they were happy. Daniella and Roberto were actively involved in church. Roberto had just received his first communion and served as an altar boy.

Jason asked her why she was afraid to return to her home country.

"Because they will kill Roberto, and they will kill me," she said, looking at Jason and then turning to me. She spoke firmly, her face and arms expressing her feelings.

"Who will kill Roberto and you?" Jason asked.

"The gangs. They wanted me to give Roberto to them and I would not, so now they will kill us."

"Can you explain what you mean?" I asked.

"Roberto came home from school one day and handed me a cell phone. He told me some men gave it to him on his walk home and told him they needed his help. Everyone knows what this means. The gangs give little boys cell phones to use to provide reports to them, like who is coming into town and where the police are. Getting a cell phone is the first step in joining the gang. Roberto told me some of the other kids at school had these cell phones too. He also told me he does not want this cell phone because the gangs are bad people. He just wants to be left alone to go to school. I told Roberto we would throw out the phone and that I would walk him to school a different way in the morning."[36]

"The next morning, I took a different road to school. I had no problem bringing him to school. In the afternoon, I walked to school to pick him up. All the kids were on the playground waiting for the school bell to ring. The principal and some teachers were watching over the kids. I saw some men talking to Roberto and some of the other second graders near the swings. The principal and teachers were right there, they were supposed to be protecting them from these men, but they did nothing. When they saw me coming, they went inside the school.

"I called Roberto over and he came. We started to walk home. I said a prayer to Jesus that the men did not follow us, I held Roberto's hand with one hand, and my rosary beads in my other hand, rubbing each bead as I prayed.

"When I saw they were not following us, I asked Roberto who they were. He said they were the bad men who gave him the cell phone. They wanted to know where it was. He told them he lost it.

"I thought we were safe, but when we were almost home, some men stepped out in front of us. They were different men, but from the same gang. There is only one gang in our town. They asked me what happened to the cell phone. I told them we must have lost it walking to school.

"They told me that Roberto was coming with them—he was theirs now."

Daniella's voice cracked and she started to cry. I handed her a tissue.

She paused to compose herself, twisting the tissue in her hand. After a pause, she continued.

"They told me if I did not give him to them, they would make me watch while they slowly cut Roberto up into pieces. And then they would make me watch while they did the same to my parents. And then they would do the same to me."[37]

Daniella started sobbing now, heavy, heaving sobs. She struggled to compose herself.

Roberto reached out and took his mom's hand. He put his head in her lap. She started to stroke his hair. I thought about asking Daniella if she would like Roberto to leave so he did not need to hear this. But I realized that would be pointless because he already *had* heard it—not only just now, but he was also there when it happened. I could also see they needed each other right now, and the simple act of patting her son's head in her lap seemed reassuring to both.

"He's just seven years old. He's a good boy," Daniella continued. "He loves Jesus and is a servant of God. I know what these men do, they come to you and take your son and he's gone. He's part of the gang. They will force him to kill, they will force him to rape, they will force him to rob and hurt others, and take other little boys from their mothers, or they would kill him. Or they might kill him anyway. The gangs kill children all the time. They owe no loyalties to anyone but the Devil. I cannot give my son to the Devil, but if I do not, they will torture and murder him. What kind of choice is that? What choice is a mother supposed to make? His life or his soul? Both choices will destroy my little boy."

"They are not getting my son," she said, jabbing her fingers at me into the air for emphasis.

"I could not fight these men. They control the town. They know where I live, and they had knives and guns and cruel hearts," Daniella said. "They control the police. My entire family would be tortured and slaughtered if I did not do as I was told, so I decided the only way we could live was to trick them. I told them we would be honored for Roberto to join them. But I told them that his grandmother was not well. I asked if Robert could have one more night at home to say goodbye to her, and then they could have him in the morning."

She paused and gave us a brief smile, pointing her finger at the sky. "God came down and saved us at that moment. They agreed and said they would be back in the morning. They said I better not be lying to them, or they would torture us in ways we could not even imagine.

"I got home and told my parents what happened. My mother cried. My father quickly left the house, telling us he would plan to get us out of there. I packed a backpack. I knew Roberto and I would need to leave, likely forever. I knew that I would likely never see my parents again after I left.

"My father came back a few hours later. He had borrowed some money from neighbors to pay for our trip to the United States. We did not have enough money to pay for their trip too. I asked him what he was going to do. He told me that he and my mother would hide in the jungle until they could figure out how to get to my uncle's house in another part of the country.

"This part of the country was controlled by another gang. It meant he and my mother would never be able to leave their house or the other gang would kill them as spies. He told me that he and my mother lived a good life, and if it was their time to die, it was God's will. But he told me that Roberto needed to live.

"A neighbor helped smuggle Roberto and me out of town in the middle of night. He had to drive on rough jungle roads to a town a few hours away that was in between gang territory. This town is dangerous because two gangs are fighting over it, but we had the highest likelihood of getting on the bus without a checkpoint from the gang. We paid the bus driver extra money to let us hide under the seat if the bus was stopped.

"We managed to get out of the country. "Only once was the bus stopped at a checkpoint. Roberto and I hid underneath a seat in the back of the bus, and luckily, the men only stepped on the bus and looked around."

"I arrived at the United States border after crossing Mexico. First, I went to the bridge, and told the official at the border that I would like asylum in America. I explained that I could not return home, or we would be murdered. The official looked at me, and then he looked at Roberto, and he told me the United States was full, and not accepting asylum seekers, so I would need to turn around and go home.[38]

"I have no home to go back to. My family is in hiding, I do not know where my mother and father are—in the jungle? At my uncle's? Dead? And if I go back, we will be murdered. Another woman saw me turned away at the border and told me there was another way into the United States. She led me to people who could take me by the river. Once I was in the United States, I flagged down the United States officials and requested asylum. I eventually ended up here. If I am released, I will go to my cousin's house in Ohio and seek asylum."

We continued the meeting. When we finished, Jason walked them out.

"Well, that's two for two," I said, looking at Jason as he came back into the room. "I never thought I would hear a daily theme of little kids being chopped up into pieces if we send them home."

He nodded. "Neither did I. Let's keep going."

I wrote in my notebook: "Daniella, 36, and Roberto, seven, arrived at a U.S. port of entry—the bridge—and requested asylum, but they were turned away. They were from Guatemala. They came by the river and requested it again."

I stood up, walked over to the list and called another name.

Chapter 9   Elena and Matteo

"A3146386WE, Elena," I called.

A woman stood up, holding her manila envelope to her chest and reaching over to take the hand of her son, a boy who looked to be about 13. She coaxed him to stand and held his hand as they walked over to us. She watched him walk, with a concerned but loving look on her face of a woman who did this a lot. Her son had a smile on his face, and looked up and out to the side as he walked toward us with a limp, his free right arm held up against his right side, with his hand slightly twisted, with his fingers bent, and his left arm limp by his side.

Jason walked over to meet them.

I looked at Elena, holding the hand of her teenage son.

"Oh man," I thought to myself. "He has special needs."

I suddenly felt cold. My sister has Down syndrome and I spent a significant amount of time over the years with children and adults with disabilities.

But given my rudimentary understanding of asylum law, I did not even know where to begin on advocating for a child who had disabilities.

Elena introduced herself and introduced us to her son, Matteo. She was 41 and from El Salvador. I reached out and shook Elena's hand and then extended my hand out to Matteo. He returned my handshake, smiling and not making eye contact. He was thin, with warm brown eyes, thick hair, and the faint hints of a mustache beginning on his upper lip.

We led them into the meeting room.

I pulled on Jason's arm and motioned for him to hold back.

"Matteo has special needs," I said.

"What?" Jason asked, surprised. "How do you know that?"

I looked at Jason, amazed he hadn't noticed. "I know," I responded. "He definitely has physical disabilities, maybe cerebral palsy? And he may also have cognitive disabilities as well, I just don't know."

"Well, if you're right, what does that mean?" Jason asked.

"I have no idea," I answered. "I don't know how disabilities are treated in their culture, what resources his community had to support his family at home, or how this could impact asylum claims in the United States. At least, we need to be mindful of it when we talk to them because Matteo has additional vulnerabilities that we need to consider. I am going to go ask for additional guidance."

I walked out into the common room and spotted one of the longtime volunteers that had worked with legal aid tapping away on a laptop on the other side of the room. He looked up and smiled as I approached. "What's up?"

"Are there special considerations that I should be mindful of if I am prepping a family with a child with special needs?" I asked quickly.

He paused and thought for a minute. "None that I know of, just do the best you can."

With no better guidance than I had before, I returned to the room and reported my conversation back to Jason.

Jason looked over at Elena and Matteo, sitting across the room together, still holding hands. I think he was beginning to realize that I might be right.

"Okay," Jason said. "Well, we'll just have to do the best we can.

Let's see what we can figure out."

Jason asked for some background information from Elena and Matteo. They were from El Salvador. Matteo was her only son. His father had left when he was young.

Jason asked what grade Matteo was in at school. Elena paused for a moment and answered that Matteo was not in school. Jason asked when Matteo left school. Elena paused again and replied that he never went to school, that he stayed at home and helped her instead.

Jason proceeded to ask them why they were afraid to return to their country.

Elena explained that she and Matteo lived in a rural area outside of town, and that while they were poor, they had been able to get by. They lived in a small house, and to support themselves she made food, and went door to door selling it in town. Matteo helped her cook and accompanied her when she sold the food. It took them a couple hours to walk to town and back every day.

I thought of Matteo and his stiff body and slow gait and thought about how hard the walk must have been for him.

Elena paused again and took a deep breath. She reached out for Matteo's hand. He put his head on her shoulder.

She explained that there was only one road she could take into and out of town. One day, not that long ago, she was walking into town and men from the local gang approached her on the road. They pushed Matteo around, calling him bad names. She begged them to stop and they finally did, but only after taking all of their food that they had made to sell in town.

Another day she was walking home with Matteo, after selling their food in town, and the gang approached her again. This time they didn't touch Matteo, but they hurled insults at him and stole all the money they had made selling their food. They told Elena that in the future, she had to pay a fee for using this road and needed to give them food and money each time she used it.

From then on, when she went into town, she had to give the gang food on the way in and money on the way out. She could not make ends meet anymore, her business was in town and there was only one road there. The gang stole so much food going into town that she had less money coming out of town, and they would get mad at them and beat Matteo. They shoved, hit, and kicked him as they made fun of him.

She stopped bringing Matteo into town. This made her sad because he had always loved going into town with her. Instead, she would leave him home alone for long hours with nothing to do and no one to watch him, which made her nervous. He was scared being left home alone, but she did not want him to be hurt.

One day, she was walking into town with the food she and Matteo had made to sell. On the way there, the gang took all the food she had to sell. She pleaded with them not to take everything or she would have nothing to sell. They took it anyway and left. She was devastated. Without money she could not buy new food to sell, or food for her and Matteo to eat. She went home because she had nothing to sell.

In the evening, she and Matteo were sitting at the house when the gang showed up at her door. They were angry that she did not come by in the afternoon and given them money. She tried to explain that the men in the morning took all her food and that she had nothing to sell, so she had nothing they could take. They did not care. They just wanted their money. They beat Elena and Matteo and ransacked their house.

They told her that she owed them money, so they were going to take Matteo to settle the debt. They laughed at this idea and grabbed him off the ground. Matteo was scared and crying. He had a bloody nose and bruises developing on his face and body.

Elena pleaded with them and told them she would have them double their money tomorrow. She told them she would make twice as much food and settle her debt on her way back from work the next day. The leader of the group stopped and looked at the others. He agreed this would work for them but cautioned her that if she did not have as much money tomorrow or if they did not come by, the gang would be back for Matteo and he would never be coming home. He shoved Matteo back down to the ground as they left.

Elena did not know if they intended to kill Matteo or make him a gang member, or something worse. But she knew that she could not give them twice the money tomorrow because she had no food to sell, so there was no way to earn the money they demanded.

Even if she had food to sell, there were not enough people in town buying it to bring in twice as much money. The gang had stolen all her food that morning, so she could not buy the ingredients needed to make the food to sell the next day. Elena explained that they did not have electricity at home, so there was no refrigerator, electric stove, or lights. Elena said she also did not have food for her and Matteo to eat.

Elena decided they had to leave. She could not pay the gang and she knew they would be back for Matteo.

"He could not go with them," she said firmly. "He would not survive. I cannot even think about what they would do to him." Matteo sat silently, his hands folded in his lap, a slight smile on his face.

"So, we fled here," she said.

They came to the United States by the river.

We continued with the rest of the meeting and when we were done I walked them out of the room. I returned to my seat and ran my hand across my face. "First an extortion/child murder case, then two kidnapping cases." I said to Jason. "Do you think all the meetings are going to be this bad?"

"I think we're only at the tip of the iceberg," he said, matter-of-factly. "We're going to have some cases easier than this, I imagine, but I also think we're going to have worse ones."

While Jason walked out to call the next family, I wrote in my notebook: "Elena, 42, and Matteo, 13, came by the river and requested asylum. They were from El Salvador."

Chapter 10   Research

When I got back to my room that night, I logged onto my computer, planning to catch up on some work, but instead I found myself researching the Northern Triangle countries and gang violence.

"Who are these gangs?" I wondered. "How do they have so much control in these countries?"

El Salvador, Honduras, and Guatemala have two primary gangs— or *maras*—that dominate in the area: Mara Salvatrucha, also called MS-13 for short, and its main rival, the "18th Street" gang. The gangs have complete or partial control over huge parts of the Northern Triangle, with an estimated 70,000 gang members.[39] The gangs control people, travel, law enforcement, government, and judges. They can determine who lives and who dies. And they are brutal.[40]

I quickly came across a Congressional Research Service[41] report discussing Central American gangs in more detail.[42] The report had been prepared at the request of Congress for members to get a better understanding of the gang problems in Central America, particularly in the Northern Triangle. I read the report and then pulled up and read the primary sources referenced in it.

Congress had considered ways in which the United States could assist Central American countries combat gang activity and wanted to understand what types of programs were most effective in supporting these governments. Congress also wanted to understand both the impact that deportations of convicted criminals from the United States to Central America had on the problem, as well as the evolving relationship between Mexican criminal organizations and Central American gangs.[43]

Gang-related violence in El Salvador, Honduras, and Guatemala made them among the deadliest countries in the world. Unlike smaller, more local gangs in other Central American countries, MS-

13 and the 18th Street were well-organized and formed local cliques that communicated with other cliques across their own countries, other Central American countries, and the United States.[44]

Both gangs originated in the United States. MS-13 was created during the 1980s by Salvadorans in Los Angeles and is reportedly active in 46 U.S. states, plus the District of Columbia. The 18th Street gang was formed in the 1960s by Mexican youth in Los Angeles and is reportedly active in 20 U.S. states.[45]

MS-13 and 18th Street appear to have got their foothold in Central America after the United States started deporting illegal immigrants, many with criminal convictions, back to the Northern Triangle region after the passage of the Illegal Immigrant Reform and Immigrant Responsibility Act of 1996. The gangs overtook local gangs already present in the region, recruited new members among the vulnerable youth in poor neighborhoods and prisons, and engaged in forced recruitment.[46]

Central American governments have struggled to address the gang problem, but the Northern Triangle countries had long histories of violent armed conflict and political repression that inhibited the development of democratic institutions and the rule of law, which could have provided stronger tools and a culture empowered to help root out criminal activity. Several socio-economic factors exacerbated the situation, including poverty, inequality, and unemployment, particularly among youth. Government policies and country culture also made it difficult to leave a gang and integrate back into society.[47]

El Salvador unsuccessfully tried repressing gangs, until it switched tactics and tried a truce with the gangs from 2012-2014. The truce temporarily reduced homicides, but made the gangs stronger, and a new president abandoned this approach in 2014 and returned to repressive tactics, paired with military support. Honduras generally relied on suppression-oriented policies toward the gangs, combined with some community-level prevention programs, while Guatemala relied on periodic law-enforcement operations to round up suspected gang members.[48]

Women and children were often targets of gang violence in Central America, murdered as a result of turf battles, jealousy, and revenge, and forced into the sex trade. People who refused to help a gang or reported a crime were often killed. Threats and harassment by gangs have led thousands of youth to stop going to school. Gangs were involved in a broad array of other criminal activities, including extortion, money laundering, and smuggling drugs and weapons.[49] I read several other reports and news articles that buttressed this explanation.

One common occurrence is that gangs force business owners to pay high extortion fees, with failure to pay often resulting in death.[50] I read story after story like Ellen's and Anthony's, where children were murdered because parents could not pay the gang's extortion fees. Rates of infanticide—or the killing of children—in the Northern Triangle countries are some of the highest in the world. I was reminded of the opening scene in the 2015 HBO documentary Cartel Land, which begins with a funeral for the young children of a farmer in Mexico who were brutally murdered because their father could not pay an extortion fee.[51]

Another common tactic is the forcible recruitment of youth into gang membership.[52] Additionally, threats and harassment by gangs have led tens of thousands of kids in the Northern Triangle to stop going to school.[53] Not only were gangs recruiting kids in school, they were recruiting them at a very young age.[54]

Women and children were often raped by gangs, and it was not uncommon for women and children to be forced into sexual slavery. In fact, gangs use sexual violence as a strategy to maintain fear and control over their territories. Rape was widespread and used by gang members to discipline girls, women, and their family members for failure to comply with the gang's demands and to demonstrate the gang's dominance over the community.[55]

Women and children—some very young children—were subjected to many forms of sexual violence by gangs in the Northern Triangle. These include forcing them to become "girlfriends" of gang members. those who resist were subjected to sexual violence and in some cases killed. The gangs also committed gang rape, including of young children, and tortured and murdered women and girls, sometimes leaving their bodies in hidden graves, and other times in public areas to provoke fear.[55]

The United States was further concerned with the gangs, the Congressional Research Services report explained, because of the record levels of unaccompanied children and families from El Salvador, Guatemala, and Honduras seeking asylum in the United States.[56, 57]

The United Nations High Commissioner for Refugees, or UNHCR, issued two informative reports addressing immigrants fleeing Central American: "Children on the Run: Unaccompanied Children Leaving Central America and Mexico and the Need for International Protection"[56] and "Women on the Run: First-Hand Account of Refugees Fleeing El Salvador, Guatemala, Honduras, and Mexico."[57] The UNHCR also issued several other publications addressing the role of other countries when immigrants sought protection at their borders.

The UNHCR concluded that "people fleeing [Northern Triangle] violence who reached the U.S. border have bona fide needs for international protection."[58] While recognizing "that it is the prerogative of States to manage the security of their borders," the UNHCR stated that "the return of persons deemed not to need international protection should take place only after their claims have been considered through due process" and that "such returns must be carried out in a manner that is orderly, safe and respectful of the dignity of the individuals and families concerned."[59]

I read the "Women on the Run" report first. The foreword explained that the world was experiencing a global refugee crisis of a magnitude not seen since World War II. While most of the world appeared focused on refugees arriving in Europe, there was a crisis occuring in Central America driving a surge of refugees to the United States that needed protection.[60] The report noted that tens of thousands of women traveling alone or with their families were fleeing a surge of violence in El Salvador, Honduras, Guatemala, and parts of Mexico.

The report complied data from interviews with more than 160 women who had fled to the United States. These women explained that they were raped, assaulted, extorted, and threatened by members of gangs. They described seeing family members murdered or abducted and watching their children being forcibly recruited by gangs. They described incidents in which gang members murdered a loved one, such as a child or spouse. Because of the gangs, the women increasingly "barricaded themselves and their children inside their homes, unable to go to school or work fearing gunfights or direct threats from armed groups."[61] Most of them saw dead bodies in their neighborhoods.[62] The report called the Northern Triangle "one of the most dangerous places on earth."[63] Nearly all the women lived in neighborhoods controlled by gangs.

The women explained that police either could not or would not protect them.[64] Relocating to another part of the country was not an option either. More than two-thirds of the women interviewed tried moving to another location in their country, but that did not help them.[65]

Women tended to flee to the United States seeking asylum either because the harm became so intolerable that they felt they had no choice but to flee, or a "particular event prompted their immediate departure, sometimes within hours of an attack occurring."[66] The trip to the United States was "a journey through hell," with many women paying huge fees to human smugglers—or coyotes—who would often beat, rape, or kill them.[67]

I turned to the other report, "Children on the Run." It explained how the significant upward trend in asylum seekers from Central America, particularly from the Northern Triangle, began in 2009, but it was not until 2011 that the United States government recorded a steep rise, which it called "the surge," in unaccompanied or separated children arriving to the United States from the Northern Triangle countries, as well as Mexico.[68]

In interviews with over 400 unaccompanied or separated children that entered the United States, the report noted how most children interviewed were forcible displaced from their home countries because they either had experienced harm or had been threatened with harm.

Nearly half of the children interviewed had been personally affected by the increased violence in the region by gangs, drug cartels and gangs, or by criminal state actors, and that when they arrived in the United States they needed "international protection." For example, one child explained as his reason for leaving: "My grandmother wanted me to leave. She told me: 'If you don't join, the gang will shoot you. If you do join, the rival gang will shoot you—or the cops will shoot you. But if you leave, no one will shoot you.'"[69]

The report noted that every state is responsible for protecting its own citizens, but "when governments are unwilling or unable to protect their citizens, individuals may suffer such serious violations of their rights that they are forced to leave their homes and often even their families to seek safety in another country." Then, the report explained, "the international community must step in to ensure that those basic rights, as articulated in numerous international and regional instruments, are respected" for these refugees.[70] Generally speaking, "[r]efugees are persons who are outside their country of origin for reasons of feared persecution, conflict, generalized violence, or other circumstances that have seriously disturbed public order and, as a result, require international protection."[71]

My research aligned with the narratives that were being told to me in the detention facility.

Chapter 11   Ana and Gabriella

"A31489OP998, Ana," I called.

A woman stood up, clutching her manila envelope, and reached over to take the hand of her daughter, a girl around 12.

In my effort to bring in the next person as quickly as possible, I realized I got out ahead of myself. While I could certainly read, Ana's name and A number, I could not speak Spanish. I could not say anything else to her that she could understand. She looked up at me expectedly, waiting for me to tell her who I was and what to do next.

I looked around for Jason, but he was nowhere to be found.

I turned to Ana. "Me llamo, Amy," I said haltingly, reaching out to shake her hand. "No hablo español."

Ana shook my hand confused. "Ana" she said, pointing to herself. She motioned to Gabriella and said "Gabriella." Gabriella gave me a small smile and reached out to shake my hand, before looking down at the ground again.

I motioned to indicate that they should come with me, and pointed toward the interview room, smiling. When we got to the room, I indicated that they should sit down.

"Un momento," I said, holding up my finger. I turned and walked back out the door, closing it behind me.

I scanned the large common area. Still no Jason, so I called one of our law firm's volunteer translators from a list of colleagues who had offered to support our efforts remotely. A woman named Sandy, who worked in our marketing department, translated for me over the phone.

Through Sandy's interpretation, I gave Ana our now standard

introduction, about who we are and why we are here, and I asked her some basic questions about herself, like where she came from and how she got here.

The translation over the phone ended up being difficult. There was a lag between each person speaking that caused awkward and confusing pauses. Because Sandy was not in the room, she did not know when to start talking and translate, and I had a feeling she was just summarizing what Ana said rather than translating word for word. In the world of being a lawyer, every specific word matters; a summary does not work. I was beginning to get really frustrated because we had lost so much time and now the phone interpretation was not working well. I had no other choice but to keep going. Ana and Gabriella's credible fear interview was tomorrow morning.

I pieced together that Ana and Gabriella were from El Salvador. They arrived in the United States around mid-June. They had spent several weeks in Mexico, unable to present themselves at a port of entry to request asylum. On some days, Mexican authorities prevented them from getting to the port. On another day, they were assaulted and robbed. When they finally presented at the port of entry the first time, they were told to come back another day. Finally, they presented again and were detained. From the border they were sent to the ice box, and then to a detention center.

Ana explained that she was a stay at home mother, and that she has two children, a son, Miguel, 20, and Gabriella, who was in middle school. Gabriella was a straight A student and played on her school soccer team. Ana explained that she had a happy marriage with her husband, that they went to church and loved God, and that they never had any problems.

I asked Ana why she was afraid to return to her county.

"Because Gabriella will die," she said.

I asked if she wanted Gabriella to leave so she did not have to hear this. Ana shook her head no and explained that Gabriella needs to stay with her.

"Can you explain what you mean when you say Gabriella would die?" I asked.

"Gabriella was at school about two months ago when I received a phone call," Ana explained. "There was a man on the other end of the line. He said they had been watching Gabriella. They said she was very pretty, and I must be proud as her mother. They said they had an eye on her because of her brother, Miguel, and that they were going to take her to punish us because her brother gave them such a hard time."[72] Tears started to well up in Ana's eyes, and she paused for a moment. I handed her a tissue. She wiped her eyes, took a deep breath and continued.

"The man on the phone said that they were going to take her on her way home from school, and the she would be theirs," Ana continued. "They said they were going to gang rape her and keep her for the gang, and if she resisted them, they would cut her up and leave her body on my doorstep."

I could hear pauses in Sandy's voice on the phone as she translated. Her voice was getting quieter as she spoke, and less confident, almost as if she could not believe what she was hearing and wondering if she had translated it correctly.

I wondered whether anyone had explained to our law firm volunteer interpreters what we would be doing in Texas so they would be prepared for what they might hear. I had read all the materials that were provided, done the training, and already sat through a few of these interviews, and it never stopped being jarring to hear someone describing to me how people wanted to murder their children.

I held up one finger to show Ana I needed a minute. I said into the phone, "Sandy, are you okay?"

She hesitated for a moment and then responded. "Yeah, I'm okay. I just didn't expect this. I'm sorry. Let's keep going."

"You're not alone," I said. "It's hard for all of us."

I turned back to Ana, picking up where we left off.

"The man on the phone threatening your daughter, do you know who it was?" I asked Ana.

Ana looked straight at me. "Someone from the gang, of course," she replied wide-eyed, like she could not believe I would have to ask this question.

"Did you call the police?" I inquired, hating to ask this question when I already knew what the answer would likely be.

Ana shook her head. "The police work for the gangs. The gangs control them. If I went to the police, it would be assured Gabriella would be murdered...or worse. I called my son Miguel. He told me to go immediately to Gabriella's school and flee. So, I did."

I glanced over at Gabriella. She was sitting on her hands, swinging her legs back and forth in the chair, looking down at the ground. She looked like the "girl next door," innocent and sweet. Her hair was pulled back into a neat ponytail, and she had straight bangs cut cleanly across her forehead. She was only 12 years old.

Ana started to fully sob now, and Gabriella jumped out of her seat to hug her. Ana was still seated in her chair, and Gabriella wrapped her mom's head in her arms and held her, putting her cheek on top of her mom's head.

"My kids would have done the same thing if I was crying," I thought. But Gabriella, just a young girl herself, was comforting her mother as she described to two strangers in a foreign country how someone planned to rape and murder her daughter.

But I was still confused about why Gabriella was being targeted and the phone translation was making the prep session progress slow.

There was a knock on the door. Jason poked his head in. "Sorry about that," he said. "Can I join you now?" He started to walk into the room and paused when he saw that Ana was crying, with Gabriella holding her tightly.

I was relieved to see Jason. I motioned for him to come in. I thanked Sandy for interpreting and brought Jason up to speed on the information I had so far. I felt bad how disjointed this session had become and I could only imagine how confused Ana and Gabriella felt.

When I was done talking, Jason sat back in his seat and opened his computer. "Okay, so it is a gang girlfriend case?" Jason said to me as he logged into his computer.

"Well, as much as you can say that for sexual slavery of a child. Let's just avoid that term altogether. It sounds consensual and it's clearly not."

"That's fine with me," Jason said.

"Alright, let's continue. This session has been so incongruent, I'm just glad you're back," I said.

"You mentioned your husband. Where was he when this call came in?" I asked Ana.

"At work," Ana said.

"And your son?" I asked.

"He's lives in the United States," she replied.

"Where in the United States?" Jason asked.

"Pennsylvania," she replied. "He was granted asylum a few years ago."

"For what?" Jason asked.

"For his political activity. He was fighting the corrupt government and police that work with the gang and they kidnapped him and tortured him. Eventually he was released, and he fled to the United States."

"Who is 'they'?" I asked.

"The gang that controlled the government and police," Ana said.

"Is this the same gang that's targeting you now?" I asked.

"Yes, it is the only gang," Ana replied.

Now the story was beginning to make sense. I was glad Jason was back to help move things along.

"Has this gang threatened you before?" Jason asked.

"Yes, after my son left," Ana explained. "They tried to set fire to our house, but we were able to put it out with the help of our neighbors. Another day, my husband was beat up on the way home from work. They said to tell our son that they could still get to us if they could not get to him."

Things settled down for a while but then we received the phone call about Gabriella.

"This is the first time Gabriella has ever been threatened," she continued. "But they do what they say they will do. So, when I received the call about Gabriella, and talked to Miguel, I left my house, picked her up from school, and came to the United States. I do not know how else to protect her. Miguel is here, and he is safe. I do not know anywhere else to bring Gabriella. There is nowhere else to go.

"Miguel is in the United States. So, I do not know why the gang would care about him or us anymore. We are not politically active.

I am a housewife, my husband has no time to do anything but work, and Gabriella is just a child. We leave the house to go to church, and school, and work, not political rallies like Miguel did."

"Has your son received any more threats from this gang since he's been in America?" Jason asked.

"I do not know," Ana said. "We never talked about it."

Jason paused and looked at me. "Should we call Ana's son and ask him? He's in the United States, so it seems easy enough to do."

I shrugged. "Sure, we might as well learn as much as we can."

Jason asked Ana if we could call her son and talk to him. She said we could and gave us his phone number. She also said that he spoke English.

I went outside to get my cell phone from the car in the parking lot and dialed the number. A man answered the phone in Spanish but switched to English when he heard my voice. I explained to Miguel that we were helping Ana and Gabriella plan for their credible fear interview, and that we were in a family detention center in Texas.

Miguel explained to me that when he was still in El Salvador, he worked for an organization trying to root out the corruption. He had been kidnapped, beaten, and threatened. He received threats that they were going to come after his family.

He was particularly worried about Gabriella's safety, because she was a girl. Others in his organization started to disappear, and members of their family were being targeted.

He explained that he received a call one day telling him that if he did not stop, they would come for Gabriella. Around the same time his best friend was kidnapped, tortured, and executed. He knew that he would likely be next. He was angry and heartbroken, so he went to the police to file a report and force them to confront their corruption.

"Normal, everyday people should not have to live in this type of fear," Miguel explained. "They would be better with no government than the government we have, who all worked for the gangs."

When he arrived at the station, a police officer took Miguel into a private room, and listened to what he had to say, but wrote nothing down. He explained that the gang controlled the entire police force, the judges, the prosecutor, and the politicians. There was nowhere to go for help. The policeman explained that he could not even write a police report. He said if he did, the gang would know, and they would go after him. They would also likely kill Miguel and hurt his family.

"The best advice the officer had for me was that I disappear," Miguel said. "If I left, he thought the gang might lose interest in me and my family. So, I disappeared. I left."

After trying to hide in a few other places in El Salvador, Miguel realized he needed to go to the United States. "I could not move freely outside," he explained. "I was in hiding in friends' and family members' houses, which put them in danger. The gangs were everywhere, all the roads and buses. Because I could not work, I was creating a financial strain on others. And I was still receiving threatening text messages and voicemails saying the gang knew how to find me or where I was. They control everything except your brain, and you have to work hard so they do not get that too.

"I threw out my cell phone, and almost immediately the family I was staying with received threatening texts. I learned later that the gangs work with the phone company and have everyone's information. I decided I had no other choice but to flee to the United States and request asylum. I received it, and now work as a brick layer in Pennsylvania."

"But I haven't been involved in any of my former political activities since I left," Miguel said. "The only thing I can think of is that I am still connected with some of my friends over Facebook. It was recently the anniversary of my best friend's death, and I posted a comment that he sacrificed himself trying to save the El Salvadorian people from corruption and evil. It was stupid. I shouldn't have said anything. But I wanted his family to know that I remembered that he died trying to improve our condition, and that I did not forget his sacrifice for our people.

"A few days later, my mother received the phone call about Gabriella. I told her she needed to leave immediately. I told her to come here to stay with me. There is nowhere else to go in El Salvador where they could not be found. Gabriella's fate, like so many other girls at home, would be sealed if she did not leave the country. I cannot stress enough the cruelty and depravity of these people. They will rape and murder children without giving it a second thought."

After finishing the call with Miguel, I went back inside the facility and rejoined the others. I looked at Gabriella, who was clasping her mother's two hands in her lap as her mother quietly cried. This sweet, young girl sitting in front of me should be at home with her family, playing soccer with her friends, studying for exams, and doing what other 12-year-old girls get to do—not sitting here in detention in the United States listening to this conversation.

We continued the interview, and when we were finished, Jason walked them out. I wrote in my notebook: "Ana, 42, and Gabriella, 12, came by the bridge. They were from El Salvador. They were requesting asylum."

Jason walked up to the list and called another name.

Chapter 12   Marie and Victoria

As Jason walked over to the list, I looked around at the women and children sitting in the waiting area. I saw a woman sitting in a chair in the outskirts of the circle, holding her baby. The woman was looking down at the floor, with her eyes closed. Her sleeping baby snuggled into her lap.

They were seated apart from the others, despite the crowded room, and the peaceful image reminded me of a sculpture of the Virgin Mary holding the infant Jesus.

Jason called out, "A31TT98739, Marie."

The woman in the chair slowly lifted her head and looked at me. I breathed in deeply. There was an incredible and immense sadness in her face. Without saying a word, she stood up, holding her still sleeping baby close to her chest, and came toward us. She clutched the manila envelope in her hand. She did not look us in the eyes as we introduced ourselves, she just nodded, eyes downcast. We led her into a room and closed the door.

I entered Marie's A number into the computer screen and brought up her file. It said she was travelling with her daughter, Victoria, who was about a year and a half. Little Victoria was clinging to her mother's chest.

Victoria had wisps of curly hair circling her head, and big beautiful brown eyes. She woke and watched intently as she peeked out at me with her head tucked under her mother's chin.

We asked Marie where she was from, and she said El Salvador in a voice barely above a whisper.

We asked her if she was travelling with anyone other than Victoria, and she said "no," again, in a voice barely above a whisper.

We asked more questions and each time, her response was barely above a whisper.

Victoria started to squirm. Marie put her down on the chair next to her, and pushed the chair in, so she could not fall over.

I waved and said, "Hola, Victoria." She looked at me through long curled eyelashes, her cheeks round and rosy. Victoria kept trying to grab her mother's manila envelope, so I tore off a couple pieces of notebook paper and gave them to her to play with. She happily crumbled them in her hand and waved them in the air.

"Do you have any other children," I asked. Marie nodded.

"A boy or girl?" I asked.

"Boy," she replied, eyes on the ground.

"How old is your son," I asked.

"Three," she said.

"Where is your son?" I asked.

Marie did not respond. She was clasping her hands tightly together. I repeated my question.

"Not here," Marie said very quietly, almost inaudibly, after a long pause.

I leaned in toward Jason. "I can't hear her. Can you?"

He shook his head. Jason apologized to Marie, explaining that we could not hear her, and asked her to speak up. She nodded.

We continued to ask her more questions for a couple hours. We could barely hear her responses, but we also couldn't understand her responses. They were often just a few words and disconnected from the question.

At this point, I was really frustrated. I leaned in to Jason and whispered, "This is taking forever and I need a break. Do you want a cup of coffee?" He nodded, so I stepped out to the breakroom to grab a bottle of water to make us some coffee.

"How's it going?" Another volunteer Ravi asked as I entered the breakroom.

I sighed. "Okay, I guess. I'm just having a frustrating session. We've been talking for a couple hours with this woman, and I can't understand what she's saying. She doesn't make sense, she doesn't answer our questions, and we can't hear her—she's talking in this low, monotone voice. Her answers are confusing and seem jumbled up and out of order, and she's getting confused by simple questions."

"She could be suffering from trauma," Ravi said, reminding me of our earlier training on this.

"Try asking simple questions—that aren't compound—speak slowly and be patient," he continued. "I would recommend starting by asking questions about her children and then seeing where it takes you."

I thanked him and went back into the room.

Jason was staring at a nearly blank computer screen of notes when I returned, so I knew he had not covered much ground while I was gone.

"I was just talking to Ravi, and he suggested that Marie might be suffering from trauma, which would explain why we cannot seem to piece together any information," I said. "We need to figure out what happened to her."

"Okay, we can try but it still might take forever," Jason said. "Marie is going to have a credible fear interview in a few days, and the interviewer is not going to take the time to walk through this with her. She only has a few minutes to explain things clearly, concisely, and most of all, audibly."

"I agree, but this might take some time," I said, thinking of Ravi's suggestions. I looked out at all the women and children waiting for their meetings and how little progress we have made so far.

Jason sighed, and ran his hands through his hair looking at his nearly blank screen. He followed my gaze to the large crowd sitting in the middle room.

"You know, something tells me something horrible happened to this woman," I said quietly. "Let's figure out what it is first and then we'll worry about how she'll do in the credible fear interview."

"Okay, I think you're right," he said. "We're all Marie and Victoria have to help them prepare for the meeting with the asylum officer, which is going to happen one way or the other, so we have to just do the best we can."

Jason paused again. "How many horrible things have we heard about things happening to children so far? But most of those were other people's kids, or threats to the ones sitting in front of us. We might have crossed over that threshold now."

I nodded. "Ravi suggested short, simple questions. That we speak slowly, and not rush. He also suggested Marie hold Victoria in her lap. He said it would help keep Marie grounded if he was holding her."

Luckily, Victoria made that easy on us. She stood up in the chair and held her arms out for her mother. Marie picked her up and pulled her into her lap.

Once Victoria was settled, Jason turned back to Marie.

"Marie, where is your son?" Jason slowly asked again.

Ultimately, we were able to piece Marie's story together just before her credible fear interview. It took us two days, and hours of talking, but we eventually learned that Marie was from a small town in El Salvador. She lived in a house down the street from her parents. She had been married, with two children, her son David, and her daughter Victoria.

One day, she was walking down the street and a man walked up to her leering. He said he wanted her to be his. He said he was going to text her a place and she needed to meet him there. She told him she was married with two babies. He told her to do as she was told.

She had never met this man in person before, but she knew who he was. He was the local gang leader, a man who was called "The Jackal." Marie continued on her way home, hoping he was just trying to scare her.

The next day she received a text message with an address and a time. She told her husband. He had also received a text message saying he needed to leave town, or he would die.

He packed up his things and left town immediately, leaving Marie with the two children.

Marie explained that she knew what this meant. The Jackal was "claiming" her. He would rape her, and likely kidnap her. She did not want anything to do with him. She just wanted to protect herself and her children. Since he had only seen her walking down the street, she thought maybe he would forget about her.

Instead of going to the place The Jackal texted, she fled into the jungle with David and Victoria. She was terrified in the jungle, but even more terrified of home. They hid for several days in the jungle, outside in the elements until they ran out of food. They were dirty, wet, hungry, and scared. They could not stay in the jungle any longer.

Marie went back home. She just planned to stay for a few minutes to grab some clean clothes for the family.

But as soon as she got home, The Jackal arrived with some of his men. He was furious and said that he would teach her to obey.

Then he tortured and murdered three-year-old David. His men held her down and made her watch, while she held his little sister Victoria.

Just before he left, The Jackal said that he would text Marie another time and place. "If you are not there," he said, "we'll come next for her." He reached out to Victoria and stroked her cheek.

Marie ran to her parents' house, carrying David's body. Her parents took him to the hospital, but it was too late, they said. David was already dead.

Marie's father collapsed in the hospital lobby sobbing. He went up to the army guard watching the hospital door and told him what happened. He shrugged. "Pay me to care," he responded, walking away.

Marie's father went to the police station to report the murder. The police would not take the report. Her father stood screaming at the police officers until neighbors finally came and dragged him away.

The next day, Marie received another text message. Again, it just had an address and a time. The Jackal had not forgotten her. When that text came in, she picked up Victoria and fled.

Marie went to two different cities to hide. In the first one she hid at a friend's house. She received another text a few days later with an address and a time. It was the address of the house she was staying in. She threw her phone out the window and fled.

Marie went to the capital city, San Salvador, and begged on the street for people to help her. She had nothing—no food, clothes, money, not even diapers for Victoria. An elderly woman took pity on her. She stopped to talk to Marie, and when she learned what had happened to them, she let Marie and Victoria hide in her apartment. In addition to shelter, she provided them with food and clean clothes. Marie learned that this woman had a daughter, but she had been kidnapped and murdered by the gangs.

A couple weeks after they arrived, Marie went outside to pick up diapers for Victoria. The store was just a short walk on a backstreet. She thought she saw one of The Jackal's men, and immediately went back to the apartment. The next morning, she woke up to find a note slid under the door. "Found you!" it read.

The woman told Marie she needed to leave the country. There was nowhere she could go where they would not find her. Marie reached out to a friend in Florida, who told her to come and stay with her in Miami and request asylum. The kind old woman gave Marie some money who then fled to the United States carrying Victoria in her arms. Shortly after crossing by the river, they were detained.

We prepared Marie for her upcoming interview. After we were done, I handed my business card to Marie and asked her to call me if she was released so that I could try to help them. I wanted to make sure Marie found a lawyer to assist with her asylum case and I was worried about Marie's mental health, especially when with Victoria. Marie took my card and nodded.

Jason walked them out of the room.

I wrote in my notebook: "Marie, 24, and Victoria, one and half, entered the United States by the river and requested asylum. Her son David, three, had been murdered."

I never heard from them again.

Chapter 13   Home

After leaving the detention facility, I sat at the airport gate, waiting to board my plane back home. My earbuds played a song on repeat, drowning out the surrounding noise and chaos at the busy airport.

My mind drifted to all the children and the horrible violence they were just trying to survive.

I thought of Caroline, seven, with her mother Sophia, held in captivity, a man holding a gun to her head in school and trying to kidnap her, and then having to flee and leave her little sister Maria behind.

I thought of Miguel, five, who was in the wrong place at the wrong time, and who had just lost his father.

I thought of sweet and playful Anthony, six, seeing his murdered playmates and who likely would be murdered if his family was sent back.

I thought of Roberto, seven, who did not want to be forced into the gang, and how the world would treat him in a few more years with hatred and disgust if he was forced into the gang.

I thought of Matteo, 13, with his special needs and the torture intended for him if he went home.

I thought of beautiful Gabriella, 12, who, rather than being at home playing soccer with her friends, was fleeing gang rape and dismemberment.

I thought of Victoria, just a year and a half, and her big brother David, just three years old, that she would never remember, and the broken mother trying to protect her.

I thought of these children and their mothers, who often endured so much physical and emotional hardship but who ultimately decided to flee when they needed to find a safe place for their children.

Each of them had survived a long and dangerous journey to get to America. They did what many parents in their situation would do in order to ensure that the children they loved survived. And they were willing to leave everything behind—their families, their friends, their homes, their jobs, their culture, their language—and risk their lives to get to the United States in the hope of being granted asylum.

They arrived in the United States and requested asylum. And they seemingly lost their names, referred to instead by their A numbers, as they bounced around in various forms of detention. They became part of a nameless and faceless mass of thousands of other people crossing the United States' southern border.

I thought how every time a new family came into our meeting room, the first thing I asked for was their A numbers. While I was focused on entering the number into the database to pull up the right file, it was still a careless way to greet these families who had encountered so many things that undermined their humanity, back in their home countries, on their way to the United States, and again after they arrived.

I stepped onto the plane distracted in thought, walked down the aisle and to my seat and sat down. I put my head back and closed my eyes, listened to the music until the plane landed back home.

On arrival my husband, Ryan, and kids were waiting outside airport security for me. I kneeled to hug the kids. My son wrapped his arms around my neck and squeezed tightly. My daughter jumped up into my arms.

As we walked to the car, holding the hands of my son and daughter, my thoughts returned to Sophia and her daughters, Caroline and Maria, who were so close in age to my children.

I turned to my husband as we drove out of the airport parking lot and said, "A family might be coming to live with us if they need to, a mother and her young daughter. We just need to be ready."

"Okay," he said as he pulled out into downtown city traffic.

Chapter 14   Release

A few days after I got back from Texas, I was on an early morning call talking to a client when another call came in.

I was standing in the front yard covered in sweat after a long run. I had been running every day, trying to process my thoughts since returning from the trip.

My phone was on the porch and I was pacing back and forth in the front yard talking into an earpiece.

I walked over and looked at the phone but did not recognize the phone number.

I answered. It was Jason. His voice rushed with excitement. Sophia was being released.

I sat down on my front porch, stunned and elated.

Jason explained that Sophia had asked that I talk to her sponsor, Pedro. Sophia and her daughter Caroline planned to live with him while they applied for asylum.

Jason gave me Pedro's phone number and I called to introduce myself. After the initial awkwardness of an unexpected phone call between two strangers, I was able to explain that I was an attorney and had met Sophia and Caroline at the detention facility in Texas. I did not know what else to say, so I simply stated that I wanted to try to help them.

Pedro thanked me and explained that any help was appreciated as there was much that needed to be done for Sophia and Caroline, and hopefully one day Sophia's other daughter Maria, to start over in America.

After I hung up, my husband Ryan pulled into the driveway and I explained the news.

I also explained that I had talked to Pedro and he seemed like a lovely person, but that I wanted to be able to offer Sophia the option of living with us if needed. Ryan agreed.

I was concerned because Sophia did not know Pedro. He was the son of an acquaintance who Sophia knew from home, and while he sounded kind, Sophia and Caroline were extraordinarily vulnerable, so I just wanted to make sure they were safe.

"When they arrive at Logan in a couple days, we need to be there," I said to Ryan. "And we need to be ready to take them into our home if they are scared or something seems off. That means we'd legally have to become their sponsors."

"Okay," he replied, nodding. "I am fine with that."

"Pedro speaks Spanish, and he's from her home town, so he would be ideal to help with the transition for them, but if something is off, we need to step in."

"I agree," Ryan said.

"Oh, and Sophia and Caroline have nothing. Absolutely nothing," I said.

"Okay," he said.

In the few days before they arrived, we gathered the basic supplies that Sophia and Caroline would need. They really had nothing, so we needed to get everything.

I had tasked Ryan and the kids with things for Caroline, and I would cover Sophia. I thought Caroline would be easier because she was seven, but they came back nearly empty handed with clothes. Unfortunately, the store did not have Caroline's size.

Luckily Ryan and the kids had much better luck with everything else. They came back with two empty backpacks and bags to hold everything, some toys for Caroline and children's picture books to help her learn English, as well as shampoo, conditioner, face wash, hairbrushes, hair elastics, among other things.

When we got home, Ryan went to pick up a cell phone for Sophia, and my sister-in-law and niece walked over for a visit. They looked at all the clothes in the living room, and my sister-in law asked if there was anything else we needed. When I explained we had been unable to find clothes for Caroline, she offered to bring us some of my niece's clothes.

A few hours later they dropped off a big bag of clothes. At the top of the bag was a puppy stuffed animal. I recognized it as my niece's favorite. "He makes me feel safe when I am scared," she explained. "I don't want Caroline to be scared."

I filled the bags and stacked them neatly next to the front door, with the stuffed puppy sitting on top, until we were ready to leave for the airport.

When my family, friends, and acquaintances learned about the imminent arrival of Sophia and Caroline, they jumped into action, passing along gift cards for clothes and groceries which I added to the bags.

Before leaving for the airport, I stood surveying the bags, thinking: I would be going to the airport to meet a woman and her daughter, who both almost died in their home country, had to leave their family behind, and then almost died again coming to the United States, who were just in jail in a new country that spoke a language they did not speak, and were now being released into a city they did not know, to live with a man they did not know...or they might be living with us.

We would all find out in a few hours.

Ryan and I headed up to the airport mid-afternoon. Sophia and Caroline's flight was supposed to land around six o'clock in the evening, and we wanted to make sure we were there when they arrived so they did not miss us. She did not have a phone, so we needed to be waiting right outside the door we thought she would exit. We checked on the flight before we left. It was on time.

After parking the car at the airport, we loaded a luggage cart with the backpacks and duffel bags and headed into the airport. I walked past the spot where I had met Ryan and the kids just a few days earlier when I was returning from Texas. At that time, I never would have thought that just a few days later I would be coming back to the same place to meet Sophia and Caroline.

We stopped at the exit door outside their gate. We were still a little early, so we popped over to a coffee shop. A man and women stood in line behind us quietly speaking in Spanish. I wondered if the man might be Pedro, but I did not know who the woman was, so I figured it likely was not him.

After we picked up our coffee and sat down, Ryan checked on the flight again. It was delayed.

We walked around the airport killing time. We found a local store and picked up sweatshirts and baseball caps for Sophia and Caroline.

We found a restaurant and ate dinner, then wandered back to the same exit an hour or so later. When we got back to the exit, I saw the same man and woman that I saw in line earlier at the coffee shop. We sat down about a dozen seats away from them, with another couple in between. Ryan and I talked to each other for a little while, and as it got later, and more people started to leave the airport, there was no one else left around us but the other couple.

I got up and walked over to them. "Excuse me, but by any chance are you Pedro?" I asked.

"Yes...Amy?" he asked uncertainly. Pedro had a ready, warm smile, and jumped to his feet as I walked up to him.

"Yes!" I said, excitedly, at first shaking his hand and then hugging him. Pedro introduced me to his companion, his daughter Jessica, and I introduced them to Ryan.

We had the chance to talk to Pedro about his life. He had emigrating from Guatemala to the United States decades ago. He had three children who lived nearby just outside the city, all United States citizens, and two granddaughters.

Pedro worked every day, and had been for years, starting with a paper route in the morning where he got up at three o'clock in the morning to roll, bag, and deliver seven different types of newspapers, before going to a job in a factory Monday through Friday from seven o'clock in the morning until six o'clock at night, and then to a job at a home improvement store on nights and weekends to re-stock shelves.

Jessica was a full-time nanny, a mother to two young girls, and her husband was a builder. They also had a family paper route, where she and her husband would also get up at three o'clock in the morning to roll and bag newspapers before her husband went out to deliver them. Sometimes their oldest daughter would join them to help.

Pedro explained that he sent money home to support his family, so he worked as many hours as possible. He was very close to his mother, Sophia's elderly neighbor.

"I offered to sponsor Sophia and Caroline and provide a place to stay in the United States while they applied for asylum," Pedro explained. "Because if I didn't, they had nowhere else to go and they were going to die."

He paused, shaking his head. "When my mother told me what Sophia and her family have been through…." He paused again. "Look, I don't have much, but I have a safe place for them to live."

Pedro paused again, lost in thought. Then he smiled. "I prayed to God for strength. If you follow his path, he will provide. God is guiding us, you know," he said, pointing his finger to the sky. "We just need to listen to him."

Our meeting was working out much better than I ever could have expected. I had been hoping for the best and prepared for the worst. But Pedro and Jessica seemed to be lovely people. They appear to be a close-knit family, and willing to share that love with strangers. It began to put my mind at ease that it appeared that Sophia and Caroline would be in a safe place, and even better, in a loving household. Pedro and Jessica's family seemed to be kind-hearted and friendly.

We quickly bonded sitting in that airport, waiting for Sophia and Caroline's plane to arrive. We were tracking the plane on our phones, and the arrival time slowly kept getting pushed back. The plane landed close to ten o'clock in the evening, four hours late, so we had plenty of time to get to know each other.

We waited anxiously by the exit after the plane landed, hoping they were not lost. This was the first time they had ever flown and navigated an airport.

About a half hour after the plane landed, Sophia walked uncertainly out the door holding Caroline's hand. The two of them had nothing with them but the familiar manila folder containing their paperwork. They wore the clothes that they had arrived in the United States wearing, but they still had on the government-issued sneakers.

Sophia's eyes scanned the faces of the people waiting outside the exit door. Her eyes met mine, and a wave of recognition crossed her face. She ran toward me and threw her arms around me.

The power of human touch is remarkable. This was the first time we could do more than shake hands. We did not have to worry about rules and prison guards, we could just hug. Sophia held onto me tight and I squeezed her back just as tight. She reached over and pulled Caroline into our hug. The three of us stood there hugging each other, not saying a word. She still did not know English and I still did not know Spanish, so we still could not talk to each other.

But in this moment, we did not need to.

I stepped back and realized I was the only face she knew. She had never met Pedro before. So, I introduced her to Pedro and Jessica and then to Ryan. Pedro translated as we talked.

Sophia was surprised that we were with Pedro and Jessica, so we explained how we met while their plane was delayed. We gave them their bags and they each put on their new baseball caps and sweatshirts and we all walked out of the airport together.

Chapter 15   Counsel

Given the interest within my law firm on the immigration issues at the United States' southern border, management had scheduled a "town hall" type meeting so the group of lawyers that had just returned from volunteering at the detention center could speak about their experiences. It was held mid-afternoon in a large conference room, with video links to our other offices. I was amazed to see a packed room that included members of our board and executive management team.

During the meeting, we each talked about our own experiences at the detention center in Texas. Of the large group that went to the detention center, many of us had similar experiences. I had come to learn that the stories of the women and children I had encountered during my time there were much like the stories that my colleagues had encountered as well. While none of the stories were good, some were particularly bad.

It was in fact the particularly bad stories that troubled us most, even long after we got home.

For me, Marie and Victoria's story and the murder of Marie's son David was the most haunting. While I gave both Marie and Sophia my phone number, I never spoke to Marie again. I prayed Marie found some help, but I was relieved to still be connected to Sophia and Caroline.

During the meeting, I was also able to make a plea for referrals to an immigration attorney that might take Sophia's asylum application case pro bono. I could take the case if needed, but I was really hoping to find an immigration attorney who specialized in asylum law.

After the meeting, we received several pledges for donations, and several offers to volunteer. It was nice to see the sense of unity that learning about our experiences brought to people, regardless of background or political affiliation.

A few days later, I was in my office sorting through some emails. Since my initial request for help finding a pro bono lawyer for Sophia and Caroline, I had received several emails and phone calls offering leads. Most of the leads ended up being dead ends, but I appreciated that people were willing to make the effort to help. I was really hoping to find an attorney specializing in immigration law, with specific experience on local asylum cases, who spoke Spanish and would take the case pro bono. I realized that was a tall ask, which is why I cast a broad plea.

An intern suddenly stuck her head in my office door, sipping on an iced coffee.

"Hey, are you still looking for a pro bono lawyer for the refugee family that you're helping?" she asked.

I looked up, surprised. "Yes, I am," I said. "Do you know one?"

"Yeah, I have a friend who's an immigration attorney. She handles asylum cases. She can help you."

"What do you mean?" I asked.

"I talked to my friend. She can take the case."

I paused. Several other people had made similar statements, and I had learned that immigration attorneys generally do not seem to take asylum cases pro bono often, so I was cautious about getting too excited.

I wanted to make sure we were on the same page, so I said, "It's pro bono. Is your friend okay with that?"

"Yup, I already talked to her."

"And she's an immigration attorney?"

"Yup," she said, sipping her iced coffee.

"And she can handle an asylum case?"

"Yup, she does this all the time. She's awesome!"

"And she lives near Sophia?"

"She is!"

"And she said she could take the case...*pro bono?*"

"That's right."

"For both the mother and her daughter?"

"Uh huh."

"And she speaks Spanish?"

"She sure does!"

I paused again. Just like that, it appears my prayers had been answered.

"This sounds amazing. Can I talk to her?" I asked, still not wanting to get my hopes up too much.

"Yup. I'll make an introduction. I'll go do that right now."

The intern left, typing into her phone as she walked, her drink tucked under her arm. A few seconds later the introduction was made, just as informally as our conversation. My phone buzzed. It was a text to me and someone else. "Hey! Introducing you to Amy so you can connect to discuss the asylum case. Thx!"

A few seconds later I received a response text from the unknown person: "Hey Amy, happy to talk anytime."

I called the attorney. She confirmed she was willing to take the case pro bono.

Just like that, Sophia and Caroline had an attorney.

Chapter 16   Visit

A few weeks after their release from the detention facility, we made plans for Sophia and Caroline to come down. Pedro's family was coming too. Around nine o'clock Saturday morning, three cars pulled up in front of our house like a motorcade and turned into the driveway. The kids had been looking out the window for the cars, eager to meet Caroline, so they heralded their arrival as Ryan and I sat on the back porch, drinking coffee and reading the morning paper.

We walked out to the driveway to greet our weekend guests. Out of the first car stepped Pedro, Sophia, and Caroline. Out of the second car stepped Pedro's daughter Jessica, her husband and two daughters, seven and four. Out of the third car stepped Pedro's other daughter and her husband. I hugged Pedro, Jessica, Sophia, and Caroline and shook hands with the others.

We stood in the driveway for a few minutes making introductions and small talk. Jessica translated my conversation for Sophia, and it was nice to hear how she had settled in. She had been checking in with Immigration and Customs Enforcement as her discharge papers required, and all had gone well. She did not need to check in again for a few months.

When Sophia met my daughter, she picked her up and hugged her tightly. My daughter was the same age as Sophia's daughter Maria that she had to leave behind. Even though she was a stranger, my daughter seemed to know Sophia was a mother who needed a hug, so she hugged her back tightly.

We stood in the driveway for another minute or two before my son reached out and tagged Caroline, yelling "you're it!" and running off. Caroline started chasing him without skipping a beat, the other kids quickly joined. Caroline did not speak English, but the kids had started playing with her as soon as she arrived. It was beautiful to see how well the game of tag served as a universal children's game.

Jessica's daughters were two beautiful and thoughtful children, wearing matching dresses, with their hair pulled back in braided pigtails. If Caroline became confused with the rules of the game the kids were playing—because they kept moving home base, or changed the game from tag to zombie—one of Jessica's daughters would quickly explain the new rules in Spanish as she ran by and Caroline would adapt without skipping a beat.

While the children played, the adults headed over to the porch for coffee. Everyone was staying for the weekend at our house, so the men brought their stuff into the house and unpacked coolers and bags of food. When they were done, they came over to the porch to join us. After just a few minutes of talking, all nervousness melted away and we chatted freely. Everyone spoke English except Sophia, but Jessica translated the conversation for her in real time.

We learned that this was the first day off Pedro had taken in eight years. Miguel, Jessica's husband, also worked three jobs, and this was the first day he had taken off in four years. They both had to ask someone to cover their newspaper shifts the next day. Apparently, to take time off, they had to pay someone to take their route, which costs more money than they made in deliveries for the day, so it was costing them both money to take the day off.

Jessica had the weekends off from being a nanny and her husband took the day off from his job as a bricklayer. Jessica's younger sister and her husband both worked part-time while they finished their college degrees.

It was a beautiful summer day and the sun lit up the green grass, still wet with dew in the yard. We heard the laughter and squealing of the kids playing in the yard as we sat on the porch, getting to know each other. Sophia and Caroline seemed to have been welcomed into Pedro's family with open arms.

After a while, we decided to head out to the beach. Everyone put on their swimsuits and we packed our little red wagon filled with beach toys and chairs.

I was the last to leave the house. I heard the screen door slam behind me as I walked down the front steps and picked up the wagon handle. There was a stream of people walking from my house to the beach. My son was up ahead walking with Pedro. Caroline was holding my hand, while Jessica walked alongside us. Sophia walked down the street in front of me, holding my daughter's hand. It was a beautiful picture. In their free hands, my daughter was holding a shovel and pail, and Caroline was holding a fishing net.

Ryan leaned over and said, "This was absolutely the right thing to do."

"What was?" I asked back, looking ahead at the group streaming across the street.

"Bringing these wonderful people into our lives," he said.

We walked down to the beach and set up chairs. The kids played in the sand for a while before Sophia got down in the sand and started making mermaid tails for the girls, decorating them with shells and seaweed. I sat down on the beach and joined her. The girls squealed with laughter as the sand piled up on their legs.

After they stood up and shook the sand off they headed to the water to wash off and decided to go swimming.

I saw Caroline quickly pull back once they got to the shore's edge and grab Sophia's arm. Sophia leaned down to ask her what was wrong, and Caroline whispered something in her ear. Pedro went over to check on them.

A minute later Pedro came over to me and Ryan. He told us that Caroline was scared to go into the water. When Sophia and Caroline had crossed the Rio Grande River into the United States, they were taken across on a leaky, overcrowded raft in the pitch black of night. At the time, Caroline was afraid she was going to fall in and drown, and now she is afraid of the water.

I looked over at this sweet little girl. Sophia was down on her knees hugging Caroline as she wiped away her tears. Their visit had been so happy and fun, that it was easy to put to the back of my mind why we were all together.

Caroline had bravely endured so much: her mother missing for long periods of time, harm to other family members, her own escape from a gunman and an attempted kidnapping, leaving her little sister behind as she fled to a foreign country, almost drowning while she crossed the river into the United States, and almost dying in the U.S. desert after coyotes robbed them. Then they were detained, put in a caged holding cell and then a detention facility. Once released, she was put on an airplane, for the first time in her life, and arrived in a foreign city to move into a house with strangers.

Now she was at my house, playing at the beach like any other kid. Her fear of the water was the first time I had seen her afraid.

"Why don't I run back to the house and grab a life preserver? We can see if that helps," Ryan offered.

"That would be great," Pedro responded, smiling appreciatively.

Ryan walked back up to the house and returned a few minutes later with a child-size life preserver. Caroline put it on and eased into the water with everyone else.

The adults formed a circle around the kids, and at first Caroline clung to Sophia. We started to pass Caroline among the adults in the circle to get her more comfortable with the water. We continued to move her around the water until her fears appeared to subside a bit. While she kept the life preserver on, she started to venture out into the middle of the circle more and laugh and splash with the other kids.

Shortly after we returned from the beach, Sophia and Jessica took over the kitchen to prepare lunch. They brought chicken and beef that had been marinating for a few days to grill, and started slicing and chopping tomatoes and onions and cutting avocados. Sophia put her hand in a tall glass and ground the avocados in a bowl to make guacamole. Jessica pulled out corn meal and oil from the bags and they started making tortillas.

Pedro and Miguel took over the grill, while Sophia and Jessica continued to slice, mix, grind, and fry food in the kitchen.

I kept offering to help but was shooed away from the kitchen and the grill.

When lunch was ready, we sat out on the deck to eat. The kids were at a table down on the lawn, while the adults sat at the table on the deck. Miguel and Pedro put out plates of grilled meat, while Jessica and Sophia put out plates of grilled vegetables, guacamole, and homemade tortillas. The food was incredible.

After lunch, I asked Sophia if I could talk to her for a minute and asked Jessica to translate. We stepped inside and sat at the dining room table.

I had met with a prominent news journalist earlier in the week and wanted to talk to Sophia about being interviewed. We sat down at the kitchen table.

"There's a famous American journalist," I started to explain, "who would like to do a story on immigration from Central America and explain to the American public why people are coming here."

I paused for a moment for Jessica to translate. Their faces remained unchanged, as they both turned to look at me again, waiting for further explanation.

"He would like to interview you." I continued.

Both Sophia and Jessica had surprised looks on their faces.

"I talked to this journalist about the detention center, and how so many people that I met with were coming to America because they were fleeing captivity, torture and death. I believe this is a story people in America need to understand better. And he agreed. He asked me to help him find people he can interview in order to help tell their stories about why they are coming to America.

"When I was at the detention center, I heard so many stories like yours—women and young children coming to the United States simply to survive. I think that it is important for people to understand that many immigrants, like you, are not just coming to the United States seeking better economic conditions, but that many times it is because to stay at home would mean that you or your children would die.

"The journalist said he could change your voice, and not show your face, so no one would know who you were," I said.

I paused for a minute to gauge their reactions. Sophia and Jessica were both looking at me surprised and confused.

I instantly regretted asking Sophia to do this. She had been through too much – all in such a short amount of time. How could I ask her to sit in front of a camera?

Sophia reached out, took my hand, and said, "I will do this for you if you would like me to."

I cringed. This is exactly what I did not want to happen—I did not want Sophia to agree to speak to a journalist for me. But I did not know how I could separate this in her mind. The request was coming from me, but it was meant to help inform the national discussion about Sophia and other immigrants.

I asked Sophia to forget about the request. Sophia had been in the United States for only a few weeks. If she could not fully make the decision on her own, because she believed it was in her best interest and that of other immigrants, I could not ask her to do the interview.

After dinner, we watched the kids chase fireflies in the yard, until they eventually curled up their tired bodies in our laps and fell asleep.

Chapter 17   Children

In just the month of May 2019—Customs and Border Protection detained approximately 144,000 migrants. While this number was below the all-time highs of the late 1990s and early 2000s, when adult Mexican men were coming across the border to work, about 70 percent of detained immigrants were families or unaccompanied children.[73] Most of them were seeking asylum. Of those, only a fraction would be successful.

The United States government had also been limiting the number of people who could present at a port of entry and request asylum, and several families had turned to more dangerous ways to cross into the United States, such as crossing the Rio Grande River, so they could request asylum.[74]

The United States provides protection to certain persons who have been persecuted or are in fear of persecution through two programs: a refugee program for persons outside the United States and, an asylum program for persons physically present or arriving in the United States. The refugee program is subject to strict caps set by the President, in consultation with Congress. For fiscal year 2019, the ceiling was set at 30,000, the lowest it has ever been, besting the previous all-time low of 45,000 set the year before (even though the number of refugees admitted in fiscal year 2018 was only half that amount).[75] Of those, about 4 percent were from Latin America.[76]

In fiscal year 2019, a total of 29,916 persons were admitted to the United States as refugees, primarily from the Congo, Burma, and the Ukraine. An additional 46,508 people were granted asylum over that same period. The leading countries of nationality for persons granted asylum were China, Venezuela, and El Salvador.[77]

In 2019, it also began to emerge in news media that families were being detained in overcrowded and unsanitary conditions. Children were the most vulnerable to these harsh conditions and long detention times.

In May 2019, Wilmer Josué Ramírez Vásquez, two years old, died after being detained by Customs and Border Protection in early April and spending about a month in a hospital, where he was diagnosed with pneumonia.

Also in May, Carlos Gregorio Hernández Vásquez, age 16, died in Customs and Border Protection custody after being diagnosed with the flu. Carlos had been initially processed in a Customs and Border Protection center with a flu outbreak. He was then held at a Customs and Border Protection facility, which was only meant to be a temporary holding cell, for well-over a week. Under the law, he should not have been there for more than three days.[78] He had come to America to help financially support his eight siblings, including a brother with special needs.[79]

Carlos and Wilmer became the sixth and seventh known children to die in U.S. government custody in 2019. By comparison, for the entire decade before this, there was not a single child death in U.S. custody.[80]

In response to these numbers, Dr. Julie Linton, co-chair of the immigrant health special interest group at the American Academy of Pediatrics, told NBC News, "Children are not like adults. They get sick more quickly and each hour of delay can be associated with serious complications, especially in cases of infectious diseases. Delays can lead to death."[81] The law requires Customs and Border Protection to transfer children to the Office of Refugee Resettlement within the Department of Health and Human Services within 72 hours unless there are "exceptional circumstances."

"We do not need to be talking about the prolonged detention of children," Dr. Linton continued. "It is dangerous."

In June 2019, an attorney from the Department of Justice appeared in an oral argument before a three-judge panel of the United States Court of Appeals for the Ninth Circuit in a case challenging the government's treatment of detained children.[82] In that case, the United States government took the position that it was not required to give soap or toothbrushes to children apprehended at the United States-Mexico border and could have them sleep on concrete floors in cold, overcrowded cells, despite a requirement that children detained by the U.S. government must be kept in "safe and sanitary" facilities.[83]

In response to the government's argument that these were "safe and sanitary" conditions, Judge William A. Fletcher questioned the government's interpretation of the requirements on the government. "Are you arguing seriously that you do not read the agreement as requiring you to do anything other than what I just described: cold all night long, lights on all night long, sleeping on concrete and you've got an aluminum foil blanket?" Judge Fletcher asked. "I find that inconceivable that the government would say that that is safe and sanitary."

Another judge, Judge A. Wallace Tashima, told the government attorney, "It's within everybody's common understanding that if you do not have a toothbrush, if you do not have soap, if you do not have a blanket, it is not safe and sanitary. Wouldn't everybody agree to that? Do you agree to that?"

The third judge, Judge Marsha Berzon, told the government attorney, "You're really going to stand up and tell us that being able to sleep isn't a question of safe and sanitary conditions?'"

Also, in June 2019, a group of lawyers went to inspect a children's detention facility outside of El Paso, Texas. The legal team interviewed 60 children at the facility and found they were being housed in poor conditions, with inadequate food, water, and sanitation.[84]

Later in June 2019, after spending two months in a migrant camp in Mexico waiting to apply for asylum in the United States after fleeing El Salvador, Óscar Alberto Martínez Ramírez, 25, tried to swim across the Rio Grande River into the United States with his 23-month-old daughter, Angie Valeria, while his wife, Angie's mother, watched from the Mexican shoreline. They were swept away in a strong current. Their bodies washed up onshore soon thereafter with Angie's arms still wrapped around her father's neck.[85]

In late June 2019, I walked past a pile of newspapers in the break area at work. I picked up a copy of the New York Times and the first article I saw was on children in the detention facilities.[86]

It was the latest in a series of daily newspaper articles discussing the treatment of migrant children being held in detention facilities. It described in detail the visit of a group of lawyers to a children's detention facility in Clint, Texas and said they found that children, some as young as five months old, had been housed with filthy clothes, in dirty diapers and with inadequate food. Children were left hungry, in unsanitary conditions, not allowed to shower, not given soap, or toothpaste to brush their teeth, or allowed to sleep in a darkened room.

The next day, I walked past the newspapers in the breakroom again. I picked up the Washington Post and read another article on children in detention.[87] It quoted several people abducted from the likes of Somali pirates and the Taliban who described being given better treatment than the detained migrant children.

In early July 2019, the Department of Homeland Security Office of Inspector General issued a management alert to the Secretary of Homeland Security, notifying the Secretary of "urgent issues that require immediate attention and action." Specifically, the alert encouraged the "Department of Homeland Security to take immediate steps to alleviate dangerous overcrowding and prolonged detention of children and adults in the Rio Grande Valley."[88]

The alert resulted from a June 2019 Office of Inspector General visit to five detention facilities and two ports of entry in the Rio Grande Valley, where the office observed conditions and reviewed compliance with Customs and Border Protection "Transport, Escort, Detention and Search," or "TEDS" standards, which govern its interaction with detained individuals. It observed serious violations of these standards, including overcrowding and prolonged detention of children, families, and adults that required immediate attention.

For example, Customs and Border Protection was holding about 8,000 detainees in custody at the time of the visit, with nearly half of them held longer than the three days generally permitted under the TEDS standards, including 1,500 people held for more than ten days.[89]

As another example, Customs and Border Protection's data reflected that about one-third of nearly 1,000 children had been held longer than the three days generally permitted under the TEDS standards and the Flores Agreement, and many had been held longer than a week.[90] At the time of the visits, there were 50 unaccompanied children younger than seven years old, and some of them had been in custody for over two weeks waiting for a transfer.

The Office of Inspector General explained that several Rio Grande Valley facilities struggled to meet other TEDS standards for children and families. Children at most of the facilities had no access to showers, changes of clothes, and were held in closed cells.[91] Thousands of children were being held in unsafe, unclean, and overcrowded conditions.

The alert further noted that overcrowding in the cells exceeded fire marshal room restrictions, oftentimes by 100 percent or more, with some adults in standing-room-only cells for weeks or more than a month, during which time they had no access to a shower.

It referred to these conditions as a "ticking time bomb."[92]

The Office of Inspector General concluded that the Department of Homeland Security "was not taking sufficient measures to address prolonged detention."[93]

On Saturday, July 6, 2019, the New York Times ran another article describing the poor conditions in a children's detention facility. It detailed the squalid and inhumane conditions of children in detention facilities in the United States, where migrant children were housed without their families. The article details outbreaks of infectious disease at the children's detention center, including scabies, shingles, chickenpox, and the flu.

The article further explained that one of the detention facilities was built to temporarily hold 100 men for just a few hours at a time, and instead it was overcrowded with hundreds of children, with as many as 700 children in the small space in the April and May timeframe, who were held average for several days on average. In interviews, a lawmaker who had visited the facility noted that agents told her that they raised concerns with their superiors about the unsafe, unsanitary, and overcrowded conditions at the facility and no one was doing anything about them. [94]

The treatment of children in detention dominated the news cycle.

A number of United Nations' agreements outline countries' responsibilities to child migrants, most notably the Convention on the Rights of the Child, which affirms that countries should not separate families and should detain children "only as a measure of last resort and for the shortest appropriate period of time."[95] The United States is a signatory, but it has not ratified the convention, and is not legally bound by its provisions.

On July 8, 2019, the new United Nations High Commissioner for Human Rights, Michelle Bachelet, said that she was "appalled by the conditions" migrants faced after they cross the southern United States border.[96] Her sentiments echoed similar sentiments her predecessor had made a year earlier.

Ms. Bachelet particularly noted the treatment of children, saying she was "deeply shocked that children are forced to sleep on the floor in overcrowded facilities, without access to adequate healthcare or food, and with poor sanitation conditions."

July 8, 2019, marked one year since I had walked into the detention center in Texas for the first time. The government's handling of the immigration crisis had not improved. In fact, it had only gotten worse.

On July 10, 2019, Time Magazine published an article summarizing the current conditions of immigrants in detention centers. The article noted: "More than 50,000 people are currently being held in ICE facilities, while approximately 20,000 are being held in Customs and Border Protection centers. More than 11,000 children are now in the custody of [Health and Human Services], which holds 'unaccompanied children' for an average of 45 days."[97]

On July 10, 2019, Yazmin Juárez, whose 19-month-old daughter Mariee died weeks after being released from a detention facility, gave testimony during a Congressional hearing saying her daughter died because of "neglect and mistreatment." Mariee had died of a viral lung infection a few weeks after being released from the custody of Immigration and Customs Enforcement.

Yazmin and Mariee had been at the same detention facility where we had worked. As I watched her mother's testimony online,[98] I remembered all the sick children we had seen during our visit. Now, with a better understanding of the overcrowded and unsanitary conditions the children were held in before they arrived at the detention facility, their sicknesses made more sense.

Chapter 18 A Year Later

Just after the Fourth of July in 2019, I emailed Sophia, inviting them down for the upcoming weekend. Later in the day Sophia sent me a text confirming she was able to come on Saturday with Pedro and Caroline.

It had been a year since Sophia and Caroline had been released from detention. Throughout the year, we texted, occasionally talked on the phone, and Ryan and I popped in to check on them when we were nearby.

Sophia could not work because she was ineligible to apply for a work permit until her asylum application was submitted, and she could not submit her asylum application until her immigration number—her A number—appeared in the immigration court computer system. Nearly a year later, it still was not there. An attorney had drafted the application and checked the computer system daily for Sophia's immigration number so the application could be submitted.

Sophia spent most of her day in Pedro's basement apartment and helping him around the house. Sponsoring an immigrant family is a significant financial burden. Pedro already worked so many jobs, and Sophia was not able to contribute to household expenses, or even to cover her and Caroline's own needs because she could not work.

Because of her isolation, she had not learned English yet. She texted or emailed me in Spanish, and I used Google Translate to read the message and respond. Caroline, however, was in school and speaking English quite well. When we FaceTimed, she could translate for us. Caroline loved arts and crafts and mailed us drawings that we hung on our refrigerator.

In the meantime, back in Guatemala, Sophia's family had returned to their home because they had nowhere else to go. They were worried for their safety, particularly Maria's. Sophia's mother stayed home with Maria, and her father and brothers only left the house to go to work. Otherwise, they were effectively prisoners in their own home. Maria was still often sick with respiratory illnesses.

While Sophia and Caroline were safe in the United States, Sophia remained in a form of purgatory. Not only was she unable to apply for a work permit, she was also unable to apply for asylum more than a year after her arrival in the United States.

Most of the time, Sofia sat at home and she waited, looking at pictures of her baby girl, Maria, who was now two. She was beginning to realize that she may not see Maria again for several more years and this realization was devastating. Sophia frequently sent me pictures of Maria, who looked a lot like her older sister Caroline.

I was looking forward to seeing them again this weekend. It would also be a nice opportunity for Sophia and Caroline to get away from the city for a few days and to catch up in person.

I had spoken to Jason a few weeks back and he mentioned that he might be staying nearby on vacation around this time, so I texted and invited him over. As luck would have it, his family was vacationing a few towns over and were able to join us for dinner.

The morning of everyone's visit, Ryan and I woke up to a calm and quiet house, permitting an introspective moment. The kids were sleeping, and the only sounds were the pleasant breeze rustling the trees outside the windows, the bright chirps of the songbirds punctuated by the sad call of a mourning dove and the cheerful call of a bobwhite.

A year ago, I was saying goodbye to my family and heading to Texas. Now, the trip was coming full circle as Sophia, Caroline, and Jason were making their way to my house.

Sophia, Caroline, and Pedro arrived mid-afternoon. Jason and his family would be arriving closer to dinner time.

The kids sat on the front porch watching for our company to arrive. They called out as a car pulled up in front and turned down the driveway. Sophia stepped out of the car and hugged me tightly as I greeted them in the driveway. The kids ran up to Caroline and dragged her out of the car to play tag. I greeted Pedro and Sophia picked up my daughter and hugged her closely, speaking to her in Spanish, kissing her cheek and patting her hair. While Sophia was always close with my daughter, I knew she also reminded Sophia of holding Maria.

Caroline ran over to me, threw her arms around me and said, "Hello, Amy. I have missed you very much." She said it clearly and confidently in English, her little girl voice sweet and high.

The adults sat down on the porch to catch up. My daughter sat in Sophia's lap while we talked.

I wanted to ask Sophia about Maria and her family's safety at home, but I did not want to talk about it in front of the kids. I pulled out my phone and used a translation app for real-time translations. Their situation at home was not good. Sophia was particularly anxious about being reunited with Maria. She explained that Maria was in danger at home, and Sophia would not be able to bring her into the United States until—if—Sophia received asylum, which could take years to resolve in any event.

Sophia showed me pictures of her family, her parents, and brothers, and sister. Tears were in her eyes as she scrolled through the pictures, and she smiled when she looked at them. They were clearly very close, and she might never see them again. This fact struck me while sitting in my own home, surrounded by my family. My mom and dad, sisters, brother, their spouses, and all my nieces and nephews all lived nearby. I saw them nearly every day. I could not imagine a world where suddenly they were not physically present.

We were messaging back and forth when Ryan walked into the room with a kayak paddle. "Who wants to go to the beach?" he asked.

It was a slightly cooler day, around 72 degrees with a strong breeze on the ocean, and we had the beach mostly to ourselves. We arrived at the beach and Sophia motioned me over for a picture in the water, with the ocean in the background. We hugged closely and smiled, as Ryan took our picture. Then everyone jumped in and we took a smiling group photo.

After some pictures, I pointed to the little yellow kayak sitting at the edge of the beach. "Caroline, would you like to try kayaking?" I asked, motioning toward the kayak. She smiled and nodded enthusiastically.

We helped her into the life preserver. This was the same life preserver she wore a year ago during our trip to the beach, when she was afraid to go into the water after her dangerous journey across the Rio Grande River into the United States.

Much had happened in a year.

Caroline was not only speaking English, but she was surer of herself and outspoken, smiling so much more than she was at this point last year.

I helped Caroline onto the kayak. A strong breeze blew, and Ryan jumped up to help steady the kayak.

"Why don't I go out with her?" Ryan offered. "I can tie our kayaks together."

He walked over and picked up the other kayak while I held Caroline at the shoreline. We tied the two kayaks together and off they went, Ryan in front pulling Caroline behind as she dipped her paddle back and forth into the water.

Sophia and I walked along the water's edge following the kayaks, watching Ryan and Caroline happily chatting away.
I was jealous of their conversation. Sophia and I had developed such a strong friendship in the past year that we had easily gotten

used to passing a phone back and forth to talk, or using a third person, or even just acting things out to communicate. But now, walking along the shore without my phone or someone to interpret, I felt sad that we could not have a conversation directly with each other.

Sophia looked over at me. I pointed to Ryan and Caroline, who were still happily chatting away, and made a heart shape with my hands.

Sophia nodded in agreement.

I pointed again to them again, then her, and then made prayer hands, "ESL, por favor!" referring to the well-known class "English as a Second Language," which teaches English to foreign language speakers in the United States.

"Yes, Amy," she said in English while nodding her head in understanding. "I will."

Ryan and Caroline turned and started to make their way back to the beach. Sophia and I turned back as well. Ryan and Caroline had beat us back, and the girls were already sitting on the beach, buried from their waists down in sand, with Pedro patiently making their mermaid tails out of the packed sand.

We laughed, and Sophia jumped in to finish the job, shooing him away. I collected shells and seaweed to decorate their tails.

We walked back to the house just before dinner time to shower and get dressed before Jason and his family arrived.

Pedro carried my daughter on his shoulders, and Sophia walked holding Caroline's hand on one side and my son's hand on the other. I looked back over at them and smiled, as I pulled the red wagon, again filled with beach toys and towels, up the hill as we walked away from the beach.

Later that evening, I walked into the kitchen and heard something sizzling on the grill on the back deck, accompanied by a delicious aroma drifting through the open windows of the house. I saw Pedro and Ryan at the grill. Sophia was making corn tortillas in the kitchen, constantly alternating between flipping the tortillas and stirring the black beans heating up on the stove. A bowl of steaming rice sat on the counter covered with a dish towel to hold in the heat.

The kids, their hair still wet from showering, ran in the front door of the house and straight out the back door, barefoot and laughing as they wove between people and furniture.

A few minutes later they called out that a car was pulling into the driveway. Jason had arrived, along with his wife and son.

I called into the kitchen, letting Sophia know that Jason was here, and we walked out to greet them in the driveway.

It had been a year since they last saw each other—when Sophia and Caroline were still at the detention facility. He was not able to hug her, and like me, just had to sit back, hands in his lap as she told us her painful story. A year later, standing in my back yard, they quickly threw their arms around each other. Caroline ran up and joined Sophia's hug with Jason too. It reminded me of the first time I had hugged them both at the airport a year ago.

We headed back to the deck and caught up on the many events of the past year, including the glacial pace of Sophia's asylum application. We sat around the deck, eating dinner and talking, like we were at a long overdue family reunion.

After Jason and his family left, the kids put on their pajamas. Caroline was going to be spending the night upstairs with the kids in their room. After we tucked them in, Sophia I settled in downstairs to talk.

"Caroline is so happy to spend time here with your family, especially your daughter. She feels like she is with her little sister Maria again," she typed into her phone and handed it to me to read. I smiled and typed back, "That makes me so happy to hear."

She wiped away tears. "She's having so much fun, she doesn't want to go home."

I was so happy to see how well Caroline was doing. She was flourishing in the United States, she had eagerly jumped into the routine at school, quickly picking up English as she played with her new friends. Caroline and my daughter had been joined at the hip throughout the day, and the sight of the two of them running by, holding hands and giggling, was heartwarming.

"Can she come down and stay for a week later this summer? The kids would love that, and she could play at the beach and fish and do summertime things with us," I asked, using the translating app on my phone.

Sophia smiled and nodded, but her eyes were sad. She was much more isolated than Caroline, stuck between two worlds, trying to help both children, but only able to help one.

"Amy, I feel stuck. Caroline is safe here and happy. But Maria needs me." She typed back.

She paused, taking a shaky deep breath.

"Maria is in danger. Caroline is safe. But I can't go to Sophia and leave Caroline here and I can't stay here with Caroline and wait years for Sophia. I don't know what to do. They are sisters. And I am their mother. They should be together with me. But instead, I am left with a choice to keep one safe and leave the other in danger. This is eating me alive."

I read her message and thought of my own two children upstairs. I did not know what to say, so I just reached out and hugged her while she cried.

A few minutes later, the girls walked in to the dining room where we had been talking.

"Excuse me, Mommy," my daughter said, stepping quietly into the room.

"Yes, baby girl?" I asked, turning toward her.

"My bed isn't cozy," she said very seriously in a low whisper.

I looked and saw Caroline standing behind her, clutching the puppy stuffed animal that my niece had picked out for her the year before.

"Oh no," I said, trying to stifle my laughter. "Do you have the same problem, Caroline?"

"Yes," she said, nodding soberly. Sophia and I laughed.

I walked the girls back upstairs. I put them back in bed and tucked them tightly under the covers.

"Is this better?" I asked.

They looked at each other, and then back at me and both nodded "yes."

I kissed them both on the forehead, turned out the light, and closed the door. They quickly fell asleep, snuggled together in bed.

A week later in mid-July 2019, Sophia's A number finally appeared in the immigration court computer system and their asylum application was submitted.

Chapter 19   Another Year Later

Sophia and Caroline came down to visit in February 2020, just before the COVID-19 pandemic emerged in the United States. Sophia made us a delicious dinner of beef, beans, rice, guacamole, roasted tomatoes, and tortillas. The smells from the kitchen wafted through the house, creating a sense of warmth and comfort on an otherwise cold winter evening.

While Sophia cooked, I played the kid's favorite game, freeze tag, in the living room. Ryan had just taken them to the candy store, and we needed to get rid of their excess gummy bear-fueled energy.

After dinner, the kids sat in the living room watching a movie. I peaked in on them, and saw my daughter and Caroline snuggled under a blanket sitting in the same chair. I smiled and closed the door so Sophia and I could talk in the dining room.

We talked about Maria, who was now nearly three and had not seen her mother and sister in nearly two years. Being reunited with Maria consumed Sophia's life for those two years.

Sophia's family back in Guatemala was still not safe and they still received threats. In just the last year, one of her brothers had been attacked and beaten unconscious on his way to work one morning. Her parents and Maria rarely left the house.

Sophia's parents had become angry with her. They said she needed to come pick up Maria and take her to America. They said Maria needed her mother and a safe place to grow up.

Sophia still owed a debt to her neighbors for lending her the money to flee to the United States. Maria also became sick several times over the past couple years with respiratory illnesses and needed to be hospitalized in Guatemala. Sophia also needed to pay for those hospitalizations. The debts kept mounting.

After years of suffering, Sophia had always been able to hold on hope that there was a better life out there for her and her children, where they could live their lives in safety. But a life of safety for Sophia and Caroline created a fractured family and left her daughter Maria in danger.

Sophia could not find peace, and I was afraid she was starting to lose hope.

That was the last time we were able to see them in person for a while because the COVID-19 pandemic hit the United States a few weeks later. Sophia finally received her work permit and was hired part-time at two local restaurants to work in the back kitchen. When the pandemic hit, she was terminated from both jobs.

The year 2020 was a difficult year for everyone, including immigrants. The COVID-19 pandemic and the government response significantly disrupted all aspects of the U.S. immigration process. From routine visas to asylum applications, nearly everything in government stopped during the pandemic.

The United States shut down its borders with Mexico and Canada. The government also put in place policies enabling it to immediately turn away people who arrived at the U.S. border without giving them the opportunity to request asylum. While there was a sharp drop in apprehensions from the previous year—about half—many of those apprehended were immediately deported.[99]

A previous policy put in place that forced asylum seekers to remain in Mexico while their asylum requests were pending was indefinitely suspended, leaving more than 20,000 people in limbo in Mexico.[100]

Despite the high risk of the pandemic, tens of thousands of people remained in immigration detention centers, contained in close quarters for long periods of time with limited access to basic sanitary necessities, like soap. Thousands of detained immigrants tested positive for COVID-19, and a number of people died.[101]

While hearings continued for detained immigrants, proceedings for non-detained immigrants were suspended for several months.

Most courts were closed from mid-March through August 2020.[102] The court closures exacerbated an already extensive backlog in asylum cases.

Sophia contacted the virus at work and became sick just after she lost her jobs. She stayed at home until she recovered, but the virus hit her hard.

Sophia and Caroline were isolated in a small basement apartment during the pandemic. Their small world became even smaller when schools were shut down and they could not leave the house. They struggled with their limited resources and isolation.

There had been no progress on the asylum application before the pandemic hit and with the pandemic-related delays, no one expects any movement in the foreseeable future.

Chapter 20   A Beacon of Hope and Safety

In fall of 2020, the New York Times obtained and reviewed a draft Department of Justice Inspector General report summarizing the findings of an investigation into the U.S. government's family separation policy. The draft report apparently made clear that President Trump, Attorney General Jeff Sessions, and Secretary of Homeland Security Kirstjen Nielsen, among others, intentionally implemented the policy of separating families from their children in an attempt to inflict emotional trauma on immigrants, despite significant concerns expressed about the ethics of the practice or the ability of the government to ensure the children's well-being.[103]

The concern about the government's ability to ensure the well-being of the children was well-placed, especially in light of the poor treatment the children received while in custody and the fact that as of fall 2020, it emerged that the U.S. government had failed to reunite hundreds of children with their parents after they were separated over two years earlier. As of October 2020, the government could not find the parents for 545 children that had been separated from their families several years earlier. The Washington Post editorial board noted that "for all intents and purposes, these children were kidnapped by the U.S. government."[104]

I sat on the back porch reading these new reports and eager for the release of the Inspector General's final report.

I thought about Sophia and Caroline, the mess of policies the U.S. government has implemented and the overall struggle the U.S. has had with immigration matters for decades.

Sophia's story is just one of so many such stories about immigrants coming to the United States seeking asylum. When they arrive, they become nameless and faceless numbers. Moved through the system, treated emotionlessly, without compassion, and often inhumanely.

Sophia's story is far from a fairy tale. She has been left to sit for years waiting for her asylum claim to be processed, uncertain about when or how she can reunite with the daughter she left behind.
But Sophia did have some fortune of her side. She escaped, made it to America, and was released from detention with her daughter Caroline and into the open arms of four strangers at the airport. She was also permitted to pursue her asylum claim.

And behind this support was a broader network of Pedro's family, and my family, and others who wanted to help. I did not realize when Sophia and Caroline were released from detention how many more people would step in to provide aid. Teachers coming in early to help Caroline with her English and schoolwork. A woman who owned a consignment shop giving me seasonal wardrobes for Sophia and Caroline. Dozens of people sent grocery store gift cards, clothing gift cards, drug store gift cards. Churches and community groups asked me what they could do to help.

Watching how eagerly and genuinely so many people stepped in to help was a sign of hope in an otherwise divisive topic in a divisive America. I thought many times throughout the last couple years that this is how America should be: a country where neighbors watch out for and help each other—and Sophia and Caroline were now our neighbors.

It is also a country of fresh starts. In America, Sophia and Caroline were not defined by the harm that had been inflicted on them or the fear that this harm might spread to others, which caused their own community to expel them. They did not live in fear of walking down the street and being kidnapped, raped, tortured, or murdered. They knew if anyone did try to hurt them, they could call the police if in danger and the police would come to help.

In America, Caroline had every opportunity to go to school and receive an education, to live in a safe environment where she could go to church, the playground and otherwise live her life freely, without thinking about her safety because it was as common and assured as the air she was breathing.

It is not only a beautiful and heart-warming testament to the strength of human character when directly faced with someone in need, but also the culture embedded in our country to enable new beginnings and fresh slates.

In reading an article on women fleeing the Northern Triangle countries, I remembered being struck that no matter the hardship the women interviewed faced in their home countries, the journey here, or once they arrived in the United States, the women spoke of the United States "as a beacon of hope and safety" and they were grateful to have arrived in the United States and for the opportunity to apply for asylum.[105]

Epilogue

Many people have asked how they could be of help on immigration matters.

There is a significant need for help on many fronts. While there is a need for lawyers, translators, and doctors, there is also a need to support immigrant families when they come to the United States, such as by donating clothes and gift certificates for food. Many of these programs are run through various religious and non-profit organizations, as well as policy work and advocacy.

Learning more about immigration matters and educating others is a powerful tool as well, so I have heavily footnoted this book to provide further information to the reader.

Acknowledgements

A number of people have led to the making of this book and deserve recognition. First and foremost, I would like to thank Sophia and her family, for sharing their experiences with me and giving me the gift of their love and friendship. I would like to thank my husband, Ryan Winmill, for his support in the journey leading to this book—from going to the family detention center on last minute notice, to welcoming Sophia and her family into our lives, to encouraging me to write this book. I would also like to thank my twin sister, Elizabeth Roma, for her valuable input into the content of the book as it was being developed. I would also like to thank my colleague T. Weymouth and my firm for always making sure we can deploy teams to the places that need help most; my parents for their love and support on this journey, and the rest of family as this book came to life; and Sachin Desai for his useful feedback during the writing process.

Notes

Epigraph

[1] "Women on the Run: First-Hand Account of Refugees Fleeing El Salvador, Guatemala, Honduras, and Mexico," United Nations High Commission on Refugees, dated 2015, available at https://www.unhcr.org/about-us/background/56fc31864/women-on-the-run-full-report.html (last accessed Feb. 12, 2021).

Prologue

[2] "FY Southwest Land Border Encounters by Month," U.S. Customs and Border Protection, last modified Feb.10, 2021, available at https://www.cbp.gov/newsroom/stats/southwest-land-border-encounters (last accessed Feb. 12, 2021).

[3] "What's happening at the U.S.-Mexico border in 5 charts," by John Gramlich and Luis Noe-Bustamante, Pew Research Center, dated Nov. 1, 2019, https://www.pewresearch.org/fact-tank/2019/11/01/whats-happening-at-the-u-s-mexico-border-in-5-charts/ (last accessed Feb. 12, 2021).

[4] "FY Southwest Land Border Encounters by Month," U.S. Customs and Border Protection, last modified Feb.10, 2021, available at https://www.cbp.gov/newsroom/stats/southwest-land-border-encounters (last accessed Feb. 12, 2021).

[5] "Fact Sheet: An Overview of U.S. Refugee Law and Policy," American Immigration Council, dated Jan. 8, 2020, available at https://www.americanimmigrationcouncil.org/research/overview-us-refugee-law-and-policy (last accessed Feb. 12, 2021).

[6] "Fact Sheet: U.S. Asylum Process," National Immigration Forum, dated Jan. 10, 2019, available at https://immigrationforum.org/article/fact-sheet-u-s-asylum-process/#:~:text=In%20fiscal%20year%20(FY)%202016,10%20percent%20to%2080%20percent (last accessed Feb. 12, 2021).

[7] "Questions and Answers: Credible Fear Screening," U.S. Citizenship and Immigration Services, last reviewed/updated Jul. 15, 2015, available at https://www.uscis.gov/humanitarian/refugees-and-asylum/asylum/questions-and-answers-credible-fear-screening (last accessed Feb. 12, 2021).

Chapter 2

[8] "Questions and Answers: Credible Fear Screening," U.S. Citizenship and Immigration Services, last reviewed/updated Jul. 15, 2015, available at https://www.uscis.gov/humanitarian/refugees-and-asylum/asylum/questions-and-answers-credible-fear-screening (last accessed Feb. 12, 2021).

[9] What can start off as self-policing can turn into criminal activity, particularly where there's a lucrative drug business to take over and a recent void after driving out the old gang. *See, e.g.,* "Toxic mix of gangs, vigilantes fuels rising Mexican violence," Associated Press, dated Jun. 21, 2019, available at https://www.apnews.com/0dd55be1b2814b60944fe87b2a105db4 (last accessed Feb. 12, 2021).

Chapter 3

[10] "Attorney General announces zero-tolerance policy for criminal illegal entry," United States Department of Justice Press Release, dated Apr. 6, 2019, available at https://www.justice.gov/opa/pr/attorney-general-announces-zero-tolerance-policy-criminal-illegal-entry (last accessed Feb. 12, 2021).

[11] "Timeline: Immigrant children separated from families at the border," by Aaron Hegarty, USA Today, dated Jun. 27, 2018, available at https://www.usatoday.com/story/news/2018/06/27/immigrant-children-family-separation-border-timeline/734014002 (last accessed Feb. 12, 2021).

[12] *Ms. L. v. United States Immigration and Customs Enforcement*, Case No.: 18cv0428 DMS (MDD), "Order Granting in Part and Denying in Part Defendant's Motion to Dismiss," dated Jun. 6, 2018, available at http://immigrationcourtside.com/wp-content/uploads/2018/06/Ms-L-v-ICE-order-6-6-18.pdf (last accessed Feb. 12, 2021).

[13] "Department of Homeland Security: Nearly 2,000 children have been separated from adults at the United States border," by John Fritze, USA Today, dated Jun. 15, 2018, available at https://www.usatoday.com/story/news/politics/2018/06/15/dhs-nearly-2-000-children-separated-adults-border/706265002 (last accessed Feb. 12, 2021).

[14] Secretary Kirstjen Nielsen Twitter Account, Tweets, dated Jun. 17, 2018, available at https://twitter.com/SecNielsen/status/1008467103857463298 (last accessed Feb. 12, 2021).

[15] *See, e.g.,* "Why do some asylum seekers cross the United States southern border between ports of entry?" Human Rights First, Fact Sheet, dated Nov. 24, 2018, available at https://www.humanrightsfirst.org/sites/default/files/US-Southern-Border-Fact-Sheet.pdf (last accessed Feb. 12, 2021).

[16] "Is it legal to cross the U.S. border to seek asylum?" International Rescue Committee, dated Mar. 1, 2019, available at https://www.rescue.org/article/it-legal-cross-us-border-seek-asylum (last accessed Feb. 12, 2021).

[17] The office of the United Nations High Commissioner for Refugees, which is the United Nations refugee agency, was created in 1950, during the aftermath of the World War II, to help millions of Europeans who had fled or lost their homes. The organization continues to protect and assist refugees around the world. See History of UNHCR, available at https://www.unhcr.org/en-us/history-of-unhcr.html (last accessed Feb. 12, 2021).

[18] "U.N. human rights chief calls Trump administration's policy on migrant children 'unconscionable,'" by Carol Morello, The Washington Post, dated Jun. 18, 2019, available at https://www.washingtonpost.com/world/national-security/un-human-rights-chief-calls-trump-administrations-policy-on-migrant-children-unconscionable/2018/06/18/5b833b5a-7306-11e8-b4b7-308400242c2e_story.html?utm_term=.80196882cc58 (last accessed Feb. 12, 2021).

[19] "Family Separation By the Numbers," American Civil Liberties Union, dated Oct. 2, 2018, available at https://www.aclu.org/issues/immigrants-rights/immigrants-rights-and-detention/family-separation (last accessed Feb. 12, 2021). Of the 2,654 children the government initially determined had been separated from their parents, nearly 200 children's parents were deported, leaving them to decide whether to see their parents again and return home, or stay in the United States without them. Family separation also matters because when parents and children are together in detention, they are more likely to remain together upon release because their cases are linked. When they are separated, that does not happen, and a parent claiming asylum for their child, who is often essential to explain why the child should be granted asylum, may be deported before that can happen.

[20] "Why Big Law is taking on Trump over immigration," by Annie Correal, New York Times, dated Nov. 21, 2018, available at https://www.nytimes.com/2018/11/21/nyregion/president-trump-immigration-law-firms.html (last accessed Feb. 12, 2021).

[21] My law firm subsequently became involved in several such cases aimed at protecting the rights of children.

[22] "Family Separation By the Numbers," American Civil Liberties Union, dated Oct. 2, 2018, available at https://www.aclu.org/issues/immigrants-rights/immigrants-rights-and-detention/family-separation (last accessed Feb. 12, 2021).

[23] In the fall of 2018, the Department of Homeland Security's inspector general released a report which stated that "DHS struggled to provide accurate, complete, reliable data on family separations." "Special Review – Initial

Observations Regarding Family Separation Issues Under the Zero Tolerance Policy," OIG-18-84, United States Department of Homeland Security, Office of Inspector General, dated Sept. 27, 2018, available at https://www.oig.dhs.gov/reports/2018/special-review-initial-observations-regarding-family-separation-issues-under-zero-tolerance-policy/oig-18-84-sep18 (last accessed Feb. 12, 2021); "Separated Children Placed in Office of Refugee Resettlement Care," HHS OIG Issue Brief, OEI-BL-18-00511, United States Department of Health & Human Services, dated Jan. 2019, available at https://oig.hhs.gov/oei/reports/oei-BL-18-00511.pdf (last accessed Feb. 12, 2021) (noting in the key takeaways: "The total number of children separated from a parent or guardian by immigration authorities is unknown. Pursuant to a June 2018 Federal District Court order, Health & Human Services had thus far identified 2,737 children presently in its care that were separated from their parents. However, thousands of children may have been separated during an influx that began in 2017, before the accounting required by the Court, and Health & Human Services has faced challenges in identifying separated children.")

[24] "United States government says it still doesn't know how many migrant children it separated," by Arit John and Jennifer Epstein, Bloomberg, dated Feb. 7, 2019, available at https://www.bloomberg.com/news/articles/2019-02-07/number-of-children-separated-at-border-still-unknown-u-s-says (last accessed Feb. 12, 2021); see also "Communication and Management Challenges Impeded HHS's Response to the Zero-Tolerance Policy," OEI-BL-18-00510, by Christi A. Grimm, Principal Deputy Inspector General, U.S. Department of Health and Human Services' Office of the Inspector General, dated Mar. 2020, available at https://oig.hhs.gov/oei/reports/oei-BL-18-00510.pdf (last accessed Feb. 12, 2021).

Chapter 4

[25] "SS St. Louis: The ship of Jewish refugees nobody wanted," by Mike Lanchin, BBC World Service, dated May 13, 2014, available at https://www.bbc.com/news/magazine-27373131 (last accessed Feb. 12, 2021).

Chapter 5

[26] See, e.g., "Why do some asylum seekers cross the United States southern border between ports of entry?" Human Rights First, Fact Sheet, dated Nov. 2018, available at https://www.humanrightsfirst.org/sites/default/files/US-Southern-Border-Fact-Sheet.pdf (last accessed Feb. 12, 2021).

[27] The Office of Inspector General for the Department of Homeland Security stated in a September 2018 that limiting the number of people allowed to seek

asylum at ports of entry leads some "who would otherwise seek legal entry into the United States to cross the border illegally." *See* "Special Review – Initial Observations Regarding Family Separation Issues Under the Zero Tolerance Policy," OIG-18-84, Office of the Inspector General, U. S. Department of Homeland Security, dated Sept. 27, 2018, available at https://www.oig.dhs.gov/sites/default/files/assets/2018-10/OIG-18-84-Sep18.pdf (last accessed Feb. 12, 2021).

[28] The Immigration and Nationality Act, § 101, "Definitions", at (a)(42)(A), 8 U.S.C. § 1101(a)(42)(A); The Immigration and Nationality Act § 208, "Asylum" at (b)(1)(A), (B)(i), 8 U.S.C. § 1158(b)(1)(A), (B)(i), available at https://uscode.house.gov/view.xhtml?req=granuleid:USC-prelim-title8-section1101&num=0&edition=prelim and https://uscode.house.gov/view.xhtml?req=granuleid:USC-prelim-title8-section1158&num=0&edition=prelim, respectively (last accessed Feb. 12, 2021).

[29] *See Matter of A-B-*, 27 I&N Dec. 316 (A.G. 2018), Interim Decision #3929, dated Jun. 11, 2018, U.S. Department of Justice, Office of the Attorney General, available at https://www.justice.gov/eoir/page/file/1070866/download (last accessed Feb. 12, 2021); "Sessions says domestic and gang violence are not grounds for asylum," by Katie Benner and Caitlin Dickerson, New York Times, dated Jun. 11, 2018, available at https://www.nytimes.com/2018/06/11/us/politics/sessions-domestic-violence-asylum.html (last accessed Feb. 12, 2021).

[30] *See* "Women on the Run: First-Hand Account of Refugees Fleeing El Salvador, Guatemala, Honduras, and Mexico," United Nations High Commission on Refugees, dated 2015, available at https://www.unhcr.org/about-us/background/56fc31864/women-on-the-run-full-report.html (last accessed Feb. 12, 2021).

[31] Per Article 1 of the Convention, "the term 'torture' means any act by which severe pain or suffering, whether physical or mental, is intentionally inflicted on a person for such purposes as obtaining from him or a third person information or a confession, punishing him for an act he or a third person has committed or is suspected of having committed, or intimidating or coercing him or a third person, or for any reason based on discrimination of any kind, when such pain or suffering is inflicted by or at the instigation of or with the consent or acquiescence of a public official or other person acting in an official capacity. It does not include pain or suffering arising only from, inherent in or incidental to lawful sanctions." The full text of the Convention is available at the United Nation Human Rights, Office of the High Commissioner's website at https://www.ohchr.org/en/professionalinterest/pages/cat.aspx (last accessed Feb. 12, 2021).

[32] "What is happening at migrant detention centers? Here's what to know," by Madeleine Joung, Time Magazine, dated Jul. 10, 2019, available at https://time.

com/5623148/migrant-detention-centers-conditions (last accessed Feb. 12, 2021). *See also* "What we know: Family separation and 'zero tolerance' at the Border," by Camila Domonoske and Richard Gonzales, NPR, dated Jun. 19, 2018, https://www.npr.org/2018/06/19/621065383/what-we-know-family-separation-and-zero-tolerance-at-the-border (last accessed Feb. 12, 2021); "The History of the Flores Settlement and its Effects on Immigration," All Things Considered, NPR, dated Jun. 22, 2018, available at https://www.npr.org/2018/06/22/622678753/the-history-of-the-flores-settlement-and-its-effects-on-immigration (last accessed Feb. 12, 2021).

[33] The Immigration and Nationality Act does not provide a framework for the family detention during removal, rather much of the legal framework stems from the Flores Settlement between the federal government and parties challenging the detention of alien minors, which the U.S. District Court for the Central District of California also entered in a case now called *Flores v. Sessions*, 862 F.3d 863, 869, 874 (9th Cir. 2017). *See* "The 'Flores Settlement' and Alien Families Apprehended at the U.S. Border: Frequently Asked Questions," by Sarah Herman Peck and Ben Harrington, Congressional Research Services, updated Sept. 17, 2018, at 1, available at https://fas.org/sgp/crs/homesec/R45297.pdf (last accessed Feb. 12, 2021).

Chapter 7

[34] Gangs frequently force business owners to pay high extortion fees, with failure to pay often resulting in death. *See, e.g.,* "Living in fear: Children displaced by gang extortion in El Salvador," by Rosarlin Hernández, UNICEF, dated Aug. 15, 2018, available at https://www.unicef.org/stories/living-fear-children-displaced-gang-extortion-el-salvador (last accessed Feb. 12, 2021); "Mafia of the Poor: Gang Violence and Extortion in Central America," International Crisis Group, dated Apr. 6, 2017, available at https://www.crisisgroup.org/latin-america-caribbean/central-america/62-mafia-poor-gang-violence-and-extortion-central-america (last accessed Feb. 12, 2021).

[35] *See, e.g.,* "Women on the Run: First-Hand Account of Refugees Fleeing El Salvador, Guatemala, Honduras, and Mexico," United Nations High Commission on Refugees, dated 2015, available at https://www.unhcr.org/about-us/background/56fc31864/women-on-the-run-full-report.html (last accessed Feb. 12, 2021).

Chapter 8

[36] Threats and harassment by gangs have led thousands of youth to abandon school, including some 39,000 in El Salvador in 2015. *See* "Gangs in Central

America," by Clare Ribando Seelke, Congressional Research Services, dated Aug. 29, 2016, at 7, available at https://fas.org/sgp/crs/row/RL34112.pdf (last accessed Feb. 12, 2021), citing Jaimi López, "Deserción Escolar por Violencia se ha Triplicado en Últimos Dos Años," ElSalvador.com, dated Jul. 19, 2016.

[37] Younger gang members are often forcibly recruited. *See* "Gangs in Central America," by Clare Ribando Seelke, Congressional Research Services, dated Aug. 29, 2016, at 2, available at https://fas.org/sgp/crs/row/RL34112.pdf (last accessed Feb. 12, 2021), citing "Unwilling participants: The coercion of youth into violent criminal groups in Central America's Northern Triangle," by Frank de Waegh, Jesuit Conference of Canada and the United States, dated 2015.

[38] *See, e.g.,* "Without a lawyer, asylum-seekers struggle with confusing legal processes," by Samantha Balaban, Sophia Alvarez Boyd, Lulu Garcia-Navarro, NPR, dated Feb. 25, 2018, available at https://www.npr.org/2018/02/25/588646667/without-a-lawyer-asylum-seekers-struggle-with-confusing-legal-processes (last accessed Feb. 12, 2021).

Chapter 10

[39] "Women on the Run: First-Hand Account of Refugees Fleeing El Salvador, Guatemala, Honduras, and Mexico," United Nations High Commission on Refugees, dated 2015, available at https://www.unhcr.org/about-us/background/56fc31864/women-on-the-run-full-report.html (last accessed Feb. 12, 2021).

[40] *See, e.g.,* "Central America's turbulent Northern Triangle," by Amelia Cheatham, Council of Foreign Relations, updated Oct. 1, 2019, available at https://www.cfr.org/backgrounder/central-americas-turbulent-northern-triangle (last accessed Feb. 12, 2021); "What lies behind Central America's gang violence: For infamous gangs like MS-13 and Barrio 18, from drug trafficking to countless homicides, brutality is the name of the game. But how did it all begin and just how much blame can be laid at the feet of the US?," by R. Viswanathan, The Wire, dated May 9, 2019, available at https://thewire.in/world/what-lies-behind-central-americas-gang-violence (last accessed Feb. 12, 2021).

[41] The Congressional Research Service is a federal legislative branch agency located within the Library of Congress that provides policy and legal analysis to Congress.

[42] "Gangs in Central America," by Clare Ribando Seelke, Congressional Research Services, dated Aug. 29, 2016, available at https://fas.org/sgp/crs/row/RL34112.pdf (last accessed Feb. 12, 2021).

[43] *Id.* at 1.

[44] *Id.* at 5 (citations omitted).

[45] *Id.* at 3, citing U.S. Department of Justice, Organized Crime and Gang Section,

"About Violent Gangs, Criminal Street Gangs" (May 12, 2015).

[46] *Id.* (citations omitted).

[47] *Id.* at 7-8 (citations omitted).

[48] *Id.* at 11-12 (citations omitted).

[49] *Id.* at 6-7 (citations omitted).

[50] *See, e.g.,* "Living in fear: Children displaced by gang extortion in El Salvador," by Rosarlin Hernández, UNICEF, dated Aug. 15, 2018, available at https://www.unicef.org/stories/living-fear-children-displaced-gang-extortion-el-salvador (last accessed Feb. 12, 2021); "Mafia of the Poor: Gang Violence and Extortion in Central America," International Crisis Group, dated Apr. 6, 2017, available at https://www.crisisgroup.org/latin-america-caribbean/central-america/62-mafia-poor-gang-violence-and-extortion-central-america (last accessed Feb. 12, 2021).

[51] For more information, *see* http://cartellandmovie.com/.

[52] "Gangs in Central America," by Clare Ribando Seelke, Congressional Research Services, dated Aug. 29, 2016, at 2, available at https://fas.org/sgp/crs/row/RL34112.pdf (last accessed Feb. 12, 2021), citing "Unwilling participants: The coercion of youth into violent criminal groups in Central America's Northern Triangle," by Frank de Waegh, Jesuit Conference of Canada and the United States, dated 2015.

[53] "Gangs in Central America," by Clare Ribando Seelke, Congressional Research Services, dated Aug. 29, 2016, at 7, available at https://fas.org/sgp/crs/row/RL34112.pdf (last accessed Feb. 12, 2021), citing Jaimi López, "Deserción Escolar por Violencia se ha Triplicado en Últimos Dos Años," ElSalvador.com, dated Jul. 19, 2016.

[54] *See, e.g.,* "Organized crime recruiting kids in Central America," Agencia EFE, dated Apr. 4, 2018, available at https://www.efe.com/efe/english/world/organized-crime-recruiting-kids-in-central-america/50000262-3572431 (last accessed Feb. 12, 2021); "Armed gangs force 'growing number' to flee north and south, in Central America," UN News, dated May 22, 2018, available at https://news.un.org/en/story/2018/05/1010362 (last accessed Feb. 12, 2021); "No Place to Hide: Gang, State, and Clandestine Violence in El Salvador," International Human Rights Clinic, Harvard Law School, dated Feb. 2007, available at https://www.wola.org/sites/default/files/downloadable/Citizen%20Security/past/Harvard_Gangs_NoPlaceToHide.pdf (last accessed Feb. 12, 2021); "Without a lawyer, asylum-seekers struggle with confusing legal processes," by Samantha Balaban, Sophia Alvarez Boyd, Lulu Garcia-Navarro, NPR, dated Feb. 25, 2018, available at https://www.npr.org/2018/02/25/588646667/without-a-lawyer-asylum-seekers-struggle-with-confusing-legal-processes (last accessed Feb. 12, 2021).

[55] "Sexual and Gender Based Violence (SGBV) & Migration Fact Sheet," Kids

in Need of Defense (KIND), Women's Refugee Commission (WRC), Latin America Working Group (LAWG) (Apr. 2018), available at https://supportkind. org/wp-content/uploads/2018/05/SGBV-Fact-sheet.-April-2018.pdf.

⁵⁶ *Id.; see also* "Forced to Flee Central America's Northern Triangle: A Neglected Humanitarian Crisis," Doctors Without Borders, dated May 2017, https:// www.doctorswithoutborders.org/sites/default/files/2018-06/msf_forced-to-flee-central-americas-northern-triangle.pdf (last accessed Feb. 12, 2021).

⁵⁶ "Gangs in Central America," by Clare Ribando Seelke, Congressional Research Services, dated Aug. 29, 2016, at 7, available at https://fas.org/sgp/crs/row/ RL34112.pdf (last accessed Feb. 12, 2021), citing Sarnata Reynolds, "It's a suicide act to leave or stay": Internal displacement in El Salvador," Refugees International, dated Jul. 30, 2015.

⁵⁷ *Id.* at 1, citing "U.S. announcement on Central America refugees highlights seriousness of situation," United Nations High Commission for Refugees press release, dated Jan. 14, 2016, available at https://www.unhcr.org/en-us/news/ press/2016/1/5697d35f6/announcement-central-america-refugees-highlights-seriousness-situation.html (last accessed Feb. 12, 2021).

⁵⁸ *Id.* at 1, citing "Increased Central American Migration to the United States May Prove an Enduring Phenomenon," Migration Policy Institute ("MPI"), by Muzaffar Chishti and Faye Hipsman, dated Feb. 18, 2016, available at https:// www.migrationpolicy.org/article/increased-central-american-migration-united-states-may-prove-enduring-phenomenon (last accessed Feb. 12, 2021) (As the MPI article explains: "More than a year and a half after the 2014 surge in child and family migration from Central America to the U.S. border reached its peak, recent flows have increasingly shown the characteristics of an enduring phenomenon, with significant policy implications for the United States and the region.")

⁵⁹ "Children on the Run: Unaccompanied Children Leaving Central America and Mexico and the Need for International Protection," United Nations High Commissioner for Refugees, dated 2014, available at https://www.unhcr. org/56fc266f4.html (last accessed Feb. 12, 2021).

⁶⁰ "Women on the Run: First-Hand Account of Refugees Fleeing El Salvador, Guatemala, Honduras, and Mexico," United Nations High Commission on Refugees, dated 2015, available at https://www.unhcr.org/about-us/ background/56fc31864/women-on-the-run-full-report.html (last accessed Feb. 12, 2021).

⁶¹ "U.S. announcement on Central America refugees highlights seriousness of situation," United Nations High Commissioner for Refugees (UNHCR), Press Release, dated Jan. 14, 2016, available at https://www.unhcr.org/en-us/news/ press/2016/1/5697d35f6/announcement-central-america-refugees-highlights-seriousness-situation.html (last accessed Feb. 12, 2021).

[62] *Id.*

[63] "Women on the Run: First-Hand Account of Refugees Fleeing El Salvador, Guatemala, Honduras, and Mexico," United Nations High Commission on Refugees, dated 2015, at Foreword, available at https://www.unhcr.org/about-us/background/56fc31864/women-on-the-run-full-report.html (last accessed Feb. 12, 2021).

[64] *Id.*

[65] *Id.* at 4.

[66] *Id.* at 2, citing World Bank Sustainable Development Department, Poverty Reduction and Economic Management Unit & Latin America and the Caribbean Region, "Crime and Violence in Central America: A Development Challenge," dated 2011, available at https://openknowledge.worldbank.org/handle/10986/2744#:~:text=The%20research%20revealed%20that%20although,severe%20toll%20on%20economic%20development (last accessed Feb. 12, 2021).

[67] *Id.*

[68] *Id.*

[69] *Id.*

[70] *Id.* at Foreword, 6, 44.

[71] "Children on the Run: Unaccompanied Children Leaving Central America and Mexico and the Need for International Protection," United Nations High Commissioner for Refugees, dated 2014, at 4-5, available at https://www.unhcr.org/56fc266f4.html (last accessed Feb. 12, 2021).

[72] *Id.* at 10.

[73] *Id.* at 8, explaining that the principal method for providing international protection to individuals unable to receive protection in their countries of origin is the 1951 Convention Relating to the Status of Refugees, and the 1967 Protocol Relating to the Status of Refugees, available at https://www.unhcr.org/en-us/3b66c2aa10 (last accessed Feb. 12, 2021).

[74] *See* "Refugees and Migrants: Definitions," The United Nations High Commissioner for Refugees website, available at https://refugeesmigrants.un.org/definitions (last accessed Feb. 12, 2021). The definition of "refugee" can be found in the 1951 Convention Relating to the Status of Refugees (Article I) and its amending protocols.

Chapter 11

[75] Central American gangs frequently target young girls for sexual violence. *See, e.g.,* "They said we would pay with our lives," Slate Magazine, Annie Hylton and Sarah Salvadore, dated Aug. 31, 2016, available at https://slate.com/human-interest/2016/08/as-central-american-gangs-target-younger-kids-

more-minors-are-fleeing-to-the-u-s.html (last accessed Feb. 12, 2021); "Central America's Children on the Run," USA for UNHCR, dated Jun. 29, 2017, available at https://www.unrefugees.org/news/central-america-s-children-on-the-run/ (last accessed Feb. 12, 2021).

Chapter 17

[76] "FY Southwest Land Border Encounters by Month," U.S. Customs and Border Protection, last modified Feb.10, 2021, available at https://www.cbp.gov/newsroom/stats/southwest-land-border-encounters (last accessed Feb. 12, 2021).

[77] "Why are migrant children dying in United States custody?" by Nicole Acevedo, NBC News, dated May 29, 2019, available at https://www.nbcnews.com/news/latino/why-are-migrant-children-dying-u-s-custody-n1010316 (last accessed Feb. 12, 2021).

[78] For fiscal year 2020 and 2021 the refugee cap was much lower. For fiscal year 2020, the cap was set at 18,000 (but only reached 11,800 refugees), and for fiscal year 2021, the cap was set at 15,000. "Trump Administration sets cap on refugees allowed into U.S. at 15,000, another record low," by Michelle Hackman, The Wall Street Journal, dated Oct. 1, 2020, available at https://www.wsj.com/articles/trump-administration-to-reduce-cap-on-refugees-allowed-into-u-s-to-record-low-18-000-11569533121?mod=article_inline (last accessed Feb. 12, 2021).

[79] *Id.*

[80] "2019 Refugee and Asylees Annual Flow Report," by Ryan Baugh, U.S. Department of Homeland Security's Office of Immigration Statistics, dated Sept. 2020, available at https://www.dhs.gov/sites/default/files/publications/immigration-statistics/yearbook/2019/refugee_and_asylee_2019.pdf (last accessed Feb. 12, 2021).

[81] "Why are migrant children dying in United States custody?" by Nicole Acevedo, NBC News, dated May 29, 2019, available at https://www.nbcnews.com/news/latino/why-are-migrant-children-dying-u-s-custody-n1010316 (last accessed Feb. 12, 2021); see *infra* note 93.

[82] "Migrant boy who died in United States custody wanted to help brother with special needs, family says," by Danielle Silva, NBC News, dated May 22, 2019, available at https://www.nbcnews.com/news/latino/migrant-boy-who-died-u-s-custody-wanted-help-brother-n1008826 (last accessed Feb. 12, 2021).

[83] "Inside a Texas Building Where the Government Is Holding Immigrant Children," by Isaac Chotiner, The New Yorker, dated Jun. 22, 2019, available at https://www.newyorker.com/news/q-and-a/inside-a-texas-building-where-the-government-is-holding-immigrant-children (last accessed Feb. 12, 2021).

[84] "Why are migrant children dying in United States custody?" by Nicole Acevedo, NBC News, dated May 29, 2019, available at https://www.nbcnews.com/news/latino/why-are-migrant-children-dying-u-s-custody-n1010316 (last accessed Feb. 12, 2021).

[85] A video of the oral argument is available at https://www.youtube.com/watch?v=Z2GkDz9yEJA&feature=youtu.be (last accessed Feb. 12, 2021).

[86] The standard of care required for children in detention facilities is set forth in the two-decade old *Flores* settlement and a law called the Trafficking Victims Protection Reauthorization Act. They require that migrant children be placed in "the least restrictive environment" or sent to live with family members. They also limit how long families with children can be detained, which courts have interpreted as 20 days. *See* "What we know: Family separation And 'zero tolerance' at the border," by Camila Domonoske and Richard Gonzales, NPR, dated Jun. 19, 2018, https://www.npr.org/2018/06/19/621065383/what-we-know-family-separation-and-zero-tolerance-at-the-border (last accessed Feb. 12, 2021); "The history of the *Flores* settlement and its effects on immigration," All Things Considered, NPR, dated Jun. 22, 2018, available at https://www.npr.org/2018/06/22/622678753/the-history-of-the-flores-settlement-and-its-effects-on-immigration (last accessed Feb. 12, 2021).

[87] "Attorneys: Texas border facility is neglecting migrant kids," by Cedar Attanasio, Garance Burke, and Martha Mendoza, AP News, dated Jun. 21, 2019, available at https://apnews.com/46da2dbe04f54adbb875cfbc06bbc615 (last accessed Feb. 12, 2021).

[88] "A father and daughter who drowned at the border put attention on immigration," by Bill Chappell, NPR News, dated Jun. 26, 2019, available at https://www.npr.org/2019/06/26/736177694/a-father-and-daughter-drowned-at-the-border-put-attention-on-immigration (last accessed Feb. 12, 2021).

[89] "We're in a dark place': Children returned to troubled Texas border facility," by Arturo Rubio and Caitlin Dickenson, The New York Times, dated Jun. 25 2019, available at https://www.nytimes.com/2019/06/25/us/john-sanders-cbp.html?utm_source=IJC+Mailing&utm_campaign=7f5333c064-EMAIL_CAMPAIGN_2019_06_26_12_40&utm_medium=email&utm_term=0_dabed701ee-7f5333c064-7425825 (last accessed Feb. 12, 2021).

[90] "'The Taliban gave me toothpaste': Former captives contrast United States treatment of child migrants," by Deanna Paul, The Washington Post, dated Jun. 25, 2019, available at https://www.washingtonpost.com/immigration/2019/06/25/taliban-gave-me-toothpaste-former-captives-contrast-us-treatment-child-migrants/?utm_term=.c627e165f730 (last accessed Feb. 12, 2021).

[91] Memorandum from Jennifer L. Costello, Acting Inspector General,

Department of Homeland Security, to Kevin K. McAleenan, Acting Secretary, Department of Homeland Security, OIG-19-51, "Management alert, DHA Needs to Address Dangerous Overcrowding and Prolonged Detention of Children and Adults in the Rio Grande Valley (Redacted)," dated Jul. 2, 2019, available at https://www.oig.dhs.gov/sites/default/files/assets/2019-07/OIG-19-51-Jul19_.pdf (last accessed Feb. 12, 2021).

[92] *Id.* at 3 n. 5, citing TEDS 4.1, which provides that "[d]etainees should generally not be held for longer than 72 hours in CBP hold rooms or holding facilities. Every effort must be made to hold detainees for the least amount of time required for their processing, transfer, release, or repatriation as appropriate and as operationally feasible."

[93] *Id.* at 5 n. 7, of the 2,669 children in the detention at the facilities during the time of the inspection, 31 percent had been there longer than 72 hours. The Inspector General reportedly explained: "The *Flores* Agreement generally permits detention of minors no longer than 72 hours, with a provision that in an influx of minors, placement should be as expeditious as possible. In addition, the Trafficking Victims Protection Reauthorization Act of 2008 requires DHS to meet this timeline unless there are "exceptional circumstances." 8 U.S.C. § 1232(b)(3), available at https://www.law.cornell.edu/uscode/text/8/1232 (last accessed Feb. 12, 2021). The *Flores* Agreement also includes a requirement that immigration officials hold minors immediately following arrest in facilities that provide: (1) access to food and drinking water; (2) medical assistance in the event of emergencies; (3) toilets and sinks; (4) adequate temperature control and ventilation; (5) adequate supervision to protect minors from others; (6) separation from unrelated adults whenever possible; and (7) contact with family members who were arrested with the minor."

[94] *Id.* at 6.

[95] *Id.* at 6-8.

[96] *Id.* at 11.

[97] "Hungry, scared, and sick: Inside the migrant detention center in Clint, Tex.," by Simon Romero, Zolan Kanno-Youngs, Manny Fernandez, Daniel Borunda, Aaron Montes and Caitlin Dickerson, The New York Times, dated Jul. 6, 2019, available at https://www.nytimes.com/interactive/2019/07/06/us/migrants-border-patrol-clint.html (last accessed Feb. 12, 2021).

[98] "Convention on the Rights of the Child," United Nation, available at https://www.ohchr.org/en/professionalinterest/pages/crc.aspx (last accessed Feb. 12, 2021).

[99] "U.N. human rights chief 'deeply shocked' by migrant detention center conditions in Texas," by Deanna Paul and Nick Miroff, The Washington Post, dated Jul. 8, 2019, available at https://www.washingtonpost.com/immigration/2019/07/08/un-human-rights-chief-deeply-shocked-by-migrant-

detention-center-conditions-texas/?utm_term=.c3b76f47d296 (last accessed Feb. 12, 2021).

[100] "What is happening at migrant detention centers? Here's what to know," by Madeleine Joung, Time Magazine, dated Jul. 10, 2019, available at https://time.com/5623148/migrant-detention-centers-conditions (last accessed Feb. 12, 2021).

[101] "Migrant mom details daughter's death after ICE detention in emotional testimony," by Daniella Silva, NBC News, dated Jul. 10, 2019, available at https://www.nbcnews.com/news/latino/migrant-mom-details-daughter-s-death-after-ice-detention-emotional-n1028471 (last accessed Feb. 12, 2021).

Chapter 19

[102] "After surging in 2019, migrant apprehensions at U.S.-Mexico border fell sharply in fiscal 2020," by Ana Gonzalez-Barrera, Pew Research Center, dated Nov. 4, 2020, available at https://www.pewresearch.org/fact-tank/2020/11/04/after-surging-in-2019-migrant-apprehensions-at-u-s-mexico-border-fell-sharply-in-fiscal-2020-2 (last accessed Feb. 12, 2021); "Fact Sheet: DHS Measures on the Border to Limit the Further Spread of Coronavirus," U.S. Department of Homeland Security, last updated Oct. 19, 2020, available at https://www.dhs.gov/news/2020/10/19/fact-sheet-dhs-measures-border-limit-further-spread-coronavirus (last accessed Feb. 12, 2021).

[103] "Special Report: The Impact of the COVID-19 on Noncitizens and Across the U.S. Immigration System, March-September 2020," by Jorge Loweree, Aaron Reichlin-Melnick and Walter Ewing, American Immigration Council, dated Sept. 30, 2020, at 21, available at https://www.americanimmigrationcouncil.org/research/impact-covid-19-us-immigration-system (last accessed Feb. 12, 2021).

[104] *Id.* at 21. The American Immigration Lawyers Association has collected summary reports prepared by U.S. Immigration and Customs Enforcement of immigrant deaths in detention. *See* "Death Detainee Reports Released by ICE," AILA Doc. No. 18121905, dated Feb. 9, 2021, available at https://www.aila.org/infonet/ice-releases-death-detainee-report (last accessed Feb.11, 2021).

[105] Special Report: The Impact of the COVID-19 on Noncitizens and Across the U.S. Immigration System, March-September 2020," by Jorge Loweree, Aaron Reichlin-Melnick and Walter Ewing, American Immigration Council, dated Sept. 30, 2020, at 21, available at https://www.americanimmigrationcouncil.org/research/impact-covid-19-us-immigration-system (last accessed Feb. 12, 2021).

Chapter 20

[106] "'We need to take away children' no matter how young, Justice Dept. officials said," by Michael D. Shear, Katie Brenner, and Michael S. Schmidt, The New York Times, dated Oct. 6, 2020 and updated on Oct. 21, 2010, available at https://www.nytimes.com/2020/10/06/us/politics/family-separation-border-immigration-jeff-sessions-rod-rosenstein.html (last accessed Feb. 12, 2021).

[107] "Let's not mince words. The Trump administration kidnapped children." Opinion by the Editorial Board, Washington Post, dated Oct. 21, 2020, available at https://www.washingtonpost.com/opinions/lets-not-mince-words-the-trump-administration-kidnapped-children/2020/10/21/9edf2e20-13b0-11eb-ba42-ec6a580836ed_story.html (last accessed Feb. 12, 2021).

[108] "Women on the Run: First-Hand Account of Refugees Fleeing El Salvador, Guatemala, Honduras, and Mexico," United Nations High Commission on Refugees, dated 2015, available at https://www.unhcr.org/about-us/background/56fc31864/women-on-the-run-full-report.html (last accessed Feb. 12, 2021).